No Short Journeys

# Cecil Robinson

# No Short Journeys

*The Interplay of Cultures in the History
and Literature of the Borderlands*

With a Foreword by Robert S. Cauthorn and
an Introduction by Reed Way Dasenbrock

The University of Arizona Press
Tucson & London

The University of Arizona Press

Copyright © 1992
The Arizona Board of Regents
All rights reserved

∞ This book is printed on acid-free, archival-quality paper.
Manufactured in the United States of America

97  96  95  94  93  92    6  5  4  3  2  1

Library of Congress Cataloging-in-Publication Data
Robinson, Cecil.
    No short journeys : the interplay of cultures in the history and
literature of the borderlands / Cecil Robinson ; with a foreword by
Robert S. Cauthorn ; and an introduction by Reed Way Dasenbrock.
      p.   cm.
    Includes bibliographical references.
    ISBN 0-8165-1270-1 (cloth)
    1. American literature—Mexican-American Border Region—History
and criticism.   2. Mexican literature—Mexican-American Border
Region—History and criticism.   3. American literature—Mexican
American authors—History and criticism.   4. Mexican-American Border
Region in literature.   5. Mexican-American Border Region—History.
I. Title.
PS277.R6   1992
810.9'86872—dc20                                  91-28170
                                                             CIP

British Library Cataloguing in Publication Data
A catalogue record for this book is available from the British Library.

Three of the essays in this volume appeared in an earlier form in the following
publications: "The Fall of the 'Big House' in the Literature of the Americas,"
in *The Arizona Quarterly* 24 (Spring 1968): 23–41; "A Creative Burst from New
Mexico: The Novels and Stories of Rudolfo Anaya," in *Puerto del Sol* 19 (Fall
1983): 125–133; and "The Culture of the Borderlands," in *Arizona's Relations
with Northern Mexico* (Phoenix, Ariz.: Arizona Academy, 1987), 121–137. They are
reproduced by permission.

*For Madeleine*

*The subject here is "the spirit behind the image" of mankind, "so small and so great, so various and so tenacious . . . where for centuries there was no such thing as a short journey."*

—Paul Horgan

# Contents

# Foreword

I received a lesson in Cecil Robinson's impact on people more than a decade ago in a dust-choked village in Sonora, a state in northern Mexico. I had spent the afternoon pushing, towing, and kicking a battered old Volkswagen Beetle that was reluctant to continue its Mexican adventure. Finally the car and I heaved out of the wasteland and approached a shuttered garage. It was late on a Friday afternoon and the mechanic had just finished cleaning up as he prepared to start his weekend. He approached me with that leisurely—and let's be honest, chilling—smile practiced by mechanics around the world. The smile that communicates, in definite terms, you don't stand a chance of getting it fixed today, buddy. Then the mechanic noticed the Arizona license plate on the car. He asked where I lived and looked bored with my response before it was delivered. I told him I hailed from Tucson. He asked if I knew Cecil Robinson. I informed him we had been friends for years. With a sudden *"Que hombre!"* the man snapped into action and threw open the doors of the garage.

The car was repaired over beer and small talk. The mechanic had never met Cecil. Instead, he was a regular listener to *"Hablemos Inglés,"* a radio program broadcast from Hermosillo, the Sonoran capital. Weekly, Cecil took to the airwaves to introduce Spanish speakers to the joys and torments of English. The mechanic's few attempts at the foreign language hinted he had not studied too hard. He said it was something else about the show that intrigued him. That something was Cecil. Soon, after a steep discount on the bill in return for a promise to send regards to Cecil, the mechanic waved and returned this traveler to the road. I have little doubt that variations on this little Friday miracle were repeated many times for Cecil's American and Mexican friends, both those he had met and those he had not. A university professor whose reach extended far beyond the classroom, Cecil made things possible and brought strangers together.

For Cecil, any border was an invitation to cross. Until his death in October 1990 he envisioned a world in which we savor our cultural distinctions. Cecil trusted that as different as we are, we could be brought together through songs, spoken stories, and the pleasures of the written word. He was ahead of his time and contemplated such things before this era, in which international cultural centers sprout on university campuses across the nation.

After serving in the Pacific during World War II, Cecil returned to Columbia University to complete his master's degree in literature and Latin American history. At the conclusion of his graduate studies, he went to Chile to direct and teach in El Instituto Chileno-Norteamericano de Cultura. In 1953 he joined the faculty of the University of Arizona and taught as he finished his doctoral dissertation for Columbia.

Cecil often found himself in his beloved Latin America over the course of his career. Whether it was directing Columbia's North American literature program in Rio de Janeiro or slipping off to Hermosillo to teach American literature, he was a bearlike, cheerful diplomat for those who hunger for a world without harsh boundaries. The broadcast of *"Hablemos Inglés"* made him a household name across Sonora. He was recognized and welcomed from the cultural center of Mexico City to the bars of South Tucson, where he sometimes prowled in hopes of learning new *norteño* ballads. Throughout northern Mexico one encounters teachers, government officials, and journalists whose lives were touched by Cecil. They all speak of him as a friend because it was Cecil's genius that people took him and his works personally.

During his academic career, Cecil served stints as the acting head of the University of Arizona English department, sat on countless committees, and received numerous awards. He sometimes found himself in the midst of stormy university battles, and in every one of them he was a voice of conciliation. He thought deeply and spoke gently, and people always listened to him. He was one of those people who commanded attention for all the right reasons. And when speaking with his fellow English professors it didn't hurt that he happened to be a dead ringer for Ernest Hemingway.

One of Cecil's most telling achievements was the establishment of the University of Arizona's Center for English as a Second Language. It is fitting that the center's acronym—CESL—sounds like his name. The center is pure Cecil: a place where students from around the world gather to learn, to enjoy different cultures, and to share their concerns.

While his professional accomplishments were substantial, Cecil came from that time before the star faculty syndrome overwhelmed universities. He was a teacher's teacher, never so truly in his element as when pacing back and forth while he lectured to a class of rapt students. He viewed teaching as ennobling and never confined his lesson plan to the classroom. Cecil peppered his conversation by freely quoting everyone from Shakespeare and James Joyce to unknown Latin American poets and Mexican farm workers. Each encounter with him taught one something unexpected. He knew a story that could illuminate almost any topic and told them all against the backbeat of his throaty laugh. Like any good storyteller, he possessed a ravenous curiosity for the stories of others as well. The effect of his uncommon blend of homespun bonhomie and academic precision could be found after every one of his classes. As his students spilled into the hallway, they wore smiles and continued the discussion among themselves—his classes never ended at the sound of the bell. Cecil did not simply break down international borders, he uprooted the fences of the mind as well.

Also after every class, there were a few students who hung about for a private word with him. Often they needed help with some problem or other. They had come to the right place. Cecil constantly tried to smooth the path for his students and colleagues. He *always* knew who to call for help, and the people he called deemed it an honor to help him help someone else. Cecil did that to you. Literally thousands of people over his long career relied on this tireless mentor, and he never turned one away.

Cecil's legacy is not confined to a particular job description. He was a champion of Latin American literature long before writers such as Gabriel Garcia Marquez made the literary world look south. Meanwhile, he brought the richness of our literature to Latin America. Whether on his own or in concert with others, he was at the forefront of early efforts at cultural exchange between the United States and Latin America. The hidden drive for all these things was the passion of the true educator. Teaching was not a job for him; it was an unalterable fact of life. Indeed he saw no division between work and life, and he succeeded at both with splendid ardor.

ROBERT S. CAUTHORN

# Introduction

One of the intellectual currents attracting considerable attention among literary critics today is the movement generally called cultural studies, and although even the proponents of cultural studies have been known to joke that no one quite knows what cultural studies is, nonetheless most work in the field has some—if not all—of the following characteristics. First, cultural studies works with material on both sides of the divide between popular and high culture, trying, if not to dismantle that line, at least not to take it for granted. Those who define themselves as studying popular culture often aggressively assert the irrelevance of high culture, thus recapitulating—if inverting—the very cultural hierarchy they seek to change. Cultural studies, in contrast, tends to assert connectedness: one understands more about both high and low culture by seeing them together. Second, cultural studies stresses the politicality of literary works, how culture in our society both reflects and creates political structures. Culture thus is not autonomous and cannot be considered in isolation from a social, political, and economic context, but neither is it simply a reflection of the context, passively determined by it. This leads to a third important aspect of cultural studies, which is that it does not dismiss cultural clichés and stereotypes in a search for authenticity and more original and powerful cultural production. The stereotype is, in fact, one of the key loci where cultural forms affect the society in which and for which they are made. One of the kinds of stereotyping of particular interest for cultural studies is cross-cultural stereotyping: how does one culture represent another? Can we break free of such distorted representations to a better understanding of others? Or are we necessarily caught up in a characteristic of representation?

Given all this, one would think that the borderlands, that part of North America where the United States and Mexico meet, would be a particularly rich site for work in cultural studies. The American Southwest and its counterpart in northern Mexico have a complex mix of Native American, Latino, and Anglo peoples, a mix that has given birth to a rich culture or complex of cultures now attracting considerable attention elsewhere. And though the area remains one of America's poorest, it is no longer the economic and political backwater it once was, given the boom in the maquiladora (or twin-plant) industries on the border and now the prospects for free trade with Mexico. The body of literature that has grown up as a result of this cultural encounter, however, is probably one of the few bodies of American literature that has not received the attention it deserves. Part of the reason for this has to do with the conventional distinction between serious and popular literature. The Southwest has had no William Faulkner, no Robert Frost, no resolutely canonical figure to compel attention to the region. The closest southwestern literature has had to such a figure is Willa Cather, who drew on her southwestern residence in writing *The Professor's House* and *Death Comes for the Archbishop.* But, of course, Cather's *patria* was Nebraska, not New Mexico, and her relation to New Mexico was that of an outsider, as much so as New Mexico's other internationally famous denizen, D. H. Lawrence. Because of its lack of a canonical figure, southwestern literature has not received the kind of analytical attention other regional literatures have received, and this suggests that some of the newer approaches connected with cultural studies may prove more suitable than traditional means to the elucidation of southwestern literature and culture.

Yet new approaches are never as new as they seem, and one way of defining the value and importance of Cecil Robinson's work is to say that he was doing cultural studies on southwestern material long before anyone knew what it was. *No Short Journeys* gathers together the essays Cecil Robinson wrote after the publication of his most substantial work, *With the Ears of Strangers,* published in 1963 and revised and republished in 1977 as *Mexico and the Hispanic Southwest in American Literature.* Both books are pioneering efforts to examine and analyze the cultural interaction in the borderlands as it has been carried forward and reflected in literature. The knowledge and erudition Robinson drew on for both works is astounding: Robinson obviously read everything written about his subject. But that is less striking than the fact that he moved, and therefore moved the study of southwestern literature, decisively beyond the belletristic approaches of earlier work on the subject, such as Lawrence Clark Powell's *Southwestern Classics* (1972). This is, if anything, more apparent in *No Short Journeys* than it is in *Mexico and the Hispanic Southwest,* since the earlier book had so much material to cover. *No Short Journeys* goes over some of the same material but more briefly, more abstractly, and therefore more analytically. Robinson thought of himself, I suspect, primarily as a literary historian, but his work also has a theoretical or methodological dimension despite the fact that Robinson made no explicit theoretical or methodological claims for his work. It is precisely because of this lack of explicitness that I would like to draw out the methodological implications latent in the studies in *No Short Journeys,* for I believe that they are fundamentally sound and that they lay out some essential principles on which the study of the literature of the Southwest can and should proceed. So, although Robinson never codified his method and probably would not have put these principles in prescriptive form, I will take the liberty of doing so. The study of the borderlands must be (1) comparative, (2) bivalent, and (3) geographical or environmental. Since what I mean by these terms may be unclear, I'd like to flesh out what they mean in the rest of this introduction, referring to the essays in *No Short Journeys* that exemplify them. Moreover, these principles have relevance to a good deal more than just the literature of a given area, and at various points I would like to suggest some ways in which they have broader relevance.

First, the study of the borderlands must be comparative. The borderlands is an area of cultural interaction, and to understand this interaction we must be prepared to look at all sides of it. Specifically, we must be able to look across both sides of the U.S.-Mexican border. The border is of particular importance because it is not just where two countries meet but where two cultures meet: Anglo North America and Hispanic Latin America. Further, one of the reasons why Robinson's work should be of interest to all scholars of American literature is that he would argue—correctly, I think—that a good deal more than the border comes into better focus if one adopts a comparative focus and method. What does one mean by American literature, after all? If it is only the literature of the United States, which is what is conventionally meant by the term, how can we justify taking the name of a hemisphere for the literary production of a single country in that hemisphere? With a single stroke we have recapitulated the entire history of *norteamericano* ignorance of (and arrogance toward) the countries to the south. Robinson was not an American exceptionalist, and he would insist that even what seems most distinctively American comes into sharper focus if we retain a hemispheric definition of America. The frontier, the strife between whites and Indians, slavery, all of these key elements in the culture and history of the United States are found in the culture and history of the rest of the Americas as well.

Robinson showed how important he thought this comparative dimension of his work was by placing first in *No Short Journeys* the essay "The Fall of the 'Big House' in the Literature of the Americas," which makes a productive comparison between Faulkner's *Absalom, Absalom!*—the story of the rise and fall of a "big house" in nineteenth-century Mississippi—and comparable works in Brazilian literature. Brazil and Mississippi may seem at some remove from the U.S.-Mexican border, but this essay provides the frame for the essays that follow, which are more focused on the Anglo-Mexican encounter in the desert Southwest. If we can see that a canonical work of southern literature can be illuminated through a comparison with Brazil, then it should be obvious that virtually any work of southwestern literature would be illuminated through a comparison with work from Latin America. Moreover, one of the points Robinson seeks to establish is that Mississippi is not as far from Latin America as we customarily think. After all, although Thomas Sutpen, the builder of the big house depicted in *Absalom, Absalom!* was raised in the Appalachian hills of backwoods Virginia, he had come to Mississippi from Haiti. The Caribbean and the American South formed an interlocking slave economy in the eighteenth and nineteenth centuries, coincidentally an aspect of southern history particularly emphasized in V. S. Naipaul's recent book about the region, *A Turn in the South* (1989). The contemporary demarcation of the area into the United States and other countries ignores much of the common political history of the area, as for centuries British America, Spanish America, and French America all included part of what is now the United States and the Caribbean. Today we live in a hemispheric American economy just as Thomas Sutpen did, and the porousness of borders shown both by Sutpen's story and by the resemblance between that story and so many others in different countries in the Americas is shown even more clearly by the border Robinson focuses on in the rest of *No Short Journeys*. The border between the United States and Mexico that looks so firm and absolute on a map has considerably less solidity and force on the ground. People trade across the border, they smuggle things across the border, and perhaps most important, they themselves move across the border. Moreover, the border itself moves: 20 percent of the population of the United States now lives on land that was once part of Mexico (and even more than that on land that once belonged to Spain). Borders—especially this one—are contingent facts, not absolute ones, and we cannot allow the abstract concept of a border to blind us to what crosses the border and to similarities between the cultures on the two sides of it.

Cecil Robinson saw this more clearly than (and well before) almost anyone else. By now, of course, many scholars of American literature at least pay lip service to the notion that we need a comparative vision of the literature of the Americas. But our departmental differentiations, our academic training, and our instinctive cast of mind are all highly bordered, highly nation-centered, still constrained by a definition of American literature as the literature of the United States. This is just as true for those scholars hoping to "open up the canon" as it is for those opposed to such an opening. We may be more receptive to work by women and American minorities than we were in the past, but for professors of American literature, just as well as for the Immigration and Naturalization Service, you still need a U.S. passport to get in the door. In this context I would argue for Robinson's work as an exemplary force for other Americanists. If one sees—as many scholars of American literature now can—the artificiality of our current conceptions of American literature and yet is unsure about how to move beyond them, the essays in *No Short Journeys* should give some guidance. Moreover, Robinson is surely correct to insist that only in such a comparative vision is southwestern literature likely to be seen as important. If one takes the literature of the United States as a coherent entity, then southwestern literature is a marginal phenomenon and will remain so, just as surely as work by American minorities. But in a comparative focus, margins and borders are meeting places and crossing points, not backwaters. The Southwest thus takes on a special importance as the place where the two Americas meet.

Of course, there is a difference between the term I have been using, the Southwest, and Robinson's term, the borderlands, and this leads to the second major methodological implication of *No Short Journeys,* one that represents a key advance beyond his earlier work. The Southwest, as used in the title *Mexico and the Hispanic Southwest in American Literature,* is a term that leaves us firmly within the United States, even if far from its center. The borderlands, in contrast, is where the United States and Mexico meet. The term *borderlands* is bivalent, by which I mean that it works well going both ways. The reason why it is important to be bivalent is this: if one is studying how a culture apprehends another, it is important to avoid accepting—consciously or unconsciously—its stereotypes. Can the study of stereotypes avoid perpetrating them? (Of course, one easy response to this is that one does not necessarily avoid stereotypes by not studying them.) Of late, there has been a real upsurge of interest in studying systems of cultural representation, and most of those engaged in such study would say, I think, that one avoids perpetuating negative representations by adopting a critical attitude toward them. This is also the apparent premise of Robinson's earlier book, particularly in its original form as *With the Ears of Strangers,* which focused on how American (i.e., *norteamericano*) images of Mexico were often biased and stereotyped. But this answer does not suffice, as the scholarly investigation of stereotypes—no matter how ostensibly critical in attitude—nonetheless runs the risk of keeping the stereotypes in circulation precisely by examining them. This is the major limitation of *With the Ears of Strangers,* and it is a real weakness in much work in cultural studies.

The only lasting antidote to the stereotypes with which we view others is to encounter the way they see us, and this is why studies of cross-cultural encounters need to be bivalent. They need to be able to cross whatever border is being studied *both ways.* If the aim is to move us beyond stereotypical systems of representation rather than simply to feel more sophisticated than those systems, then we need to try to see ourselves as others see us as well as (or rather, as a means of) examining critically the way we see others. Every scholar studying Isak Dinesen ought to know the work of Ngugi wa Thiong'o; every scholar studying Rudyard Kipling ought to know the work of R. K. Narayan. This principle of bivalence is crucial to *No Short Journeys.* A number of the essays continue the purpose of *With the Ears of Strangers,* which is to study American images of Mexico, to study how the encounter with Mexico has shaped the culture of the United States in terms of both popular stereotypes and high culture. But other essays move toward the more challenging project of trying to see how Latin American culture views and represents North American culture. In keeping with this, the essay "Flag of Illusion: The Texas Revolution as a Conflict of Cultures" tries to show both how Anglo Texans viewed Mexico and how the Mexicans viewed the invading gringos. This is an interest Robinson also pursued elsewhere, in editing and translating a fascinating collection of material written by Mexican writers on the Mexican-American War, *The View from Chapultepec* (University of Arizona Press, 1989). Robinson's effort to give us that view by writing *No Short Journeys* and editing *The View from Chapultepec* is an example worth the attention of all scholars doing cross-cultural work.

The final point that I find admirable and exemplary in Robinson's discussion is his attention to what I would like to call the geography of literature. The Southwest is a place where the constraints of nature are palpable and powerful. Wordsworth would never have written that "Nature never did betray / The heart that loved her" if he had been to this part of the world. This does not mean that man is without power over nature, whether for good or ill; anyone who crosses the border between the United States and Mexico sees how differently the two countries have shaped their environments, and anyone who goes to an Indian reservation or a pueblo inside the United States has the same point driven home in a different way. But environment and geography are powerful here in ways one cannot ignore, and this insight is what lies behind the essay "Through the Southwest—By Road, Rail, and Waterway." What might seem at first glance to be a pedestrian, even pedantic, concern with how transportation systems are reflected in the literature of the region is in fact a penetrating insight into an important aspect of literature.

In an age in which we call pieces of writing texts, we have to a large extent lost sight not just of the physicality of writing but even more of the way literary works refer to and often are shaped by the physicality of the world. When Jane Austen began to write *Mansfield Park,* she wrote her sister Cassandra, asking her if the county of Northamptonshire, where the bulk of the novel was to be set, "is a country of Hedgerows." Her final novel, *Persuasion,* has a scene in which the protagonist, Anne Elliott, is sitting on one side of a hedgerow and hears part of a private conversation about her between two people walking on the other side. I suspect she asked her sister about hedgerows in Northamptonshire when writing *Mansfield Park* because she was contemplating including a comparable scene in that earlier novel. However, since Northamptonshire was not "a country of Hedgerows," there is no such scene in the novel. A seemingly trivial fact about geography determined in some measure the events of the novel. Similarly, no one can understand the dynamic of Rudolfo Anaya's novel *Bless Me, Ultima* unless he or she grasps the physical and psychological difference between the *llano* and the valley, a difference that helps structure the sense of self of the young protagonist, Antonio. Rudolfo Anaya does not translate *llano* in his work as "plain," because he wants to insist on the absolute specificity of the term. He wants his readers to know something (and to know that they need to know something) about the geography of New Mexico in order to understand the characters in his work. We need a criticism that is responsive to these details, a criticism that can explain the chestnut trees and swans of Yeats's poetry by the existence of chestnuts and swans in the west of Ireland without reducing literature to a code crackable only by those with local knowledge. This is not as developed an aspect of *No Short Journeys* as the others I have touched on, but it is one I consider quite important. Another way of putting this is to say that a work like *Bless Me, Ultima* is a window onto a culture, a culture with geographical, historical, and political dimensions, and we need a criticism capable of registering those dimensions without reducing the literary work to simply an act of reference. There is, of course, a powerful movement in American education to incorporate into the curriculum "texts" from other cultures, but as long as we view them as texts, we are not going to get all the value we could from their study.

My mention of the work of Rudolfo Anaya here is not accidental, for Anaya is the subject of one of the two chapters in *No Short Journeys* devoted to Chicano writers. Indeed, another important way in which *No Short Journeys* represents a step beyond Robinson's earlier work is the greater prominence it gives to Chicano writing. The 1977 revision of *With the Ears of Strangers—Mexico and the Hispanic Southwest in American Literature*—does include a chapter on Chicano writing. But though it is a valuable chapter, it fits a little oddly into the thrust of the rest of the work. *Mexico and the Hispanic Southwest* is primarily a depiction of the encounter between the two opposites of Mexico and the United States, and this makes it hard to shift focus to studying works and writers who connect these supposed opposites. But the ability of Chicano writers to bridge the gap between the United States and Latin America is precisely why Chicano literature came to be of such importance to Robinson's way of seeing the borderlands. His insistence on seeing Chicano writing as existing within a larger southwestern or border context stands at some remove from most academic work on Chicano literature, which presents it as a coherent and isolated body of literature. But I think Robinson's approach makes Chicano literature a more interesting and more important phenomenon.

It is in keeping with this that *No Short Journeys* ends with two chapters on the Chicano writers Miguel Mendez and Rudolfo Anaya and a final chapter, "The Culture of the Borderlands," which argues that there has been a third culture formed on the border, no longer cross-cultural but genuinely bicultural, neither Latino nor Anglo but a combination of both. I find Robinson's depiction of this new culture overly optimistic, overly generous in its assumption of willingness of Anglos to lose the traditional Anglo cultural identity. Robinson was perhaps so willing to embrace this new synthesis that he overestimated the willingness of others to do the same. But whatever the empirical validity of the portrait he draws, it certainly seems like a valid ideal, and Robinson is also correct in pointing to the works of Chicano literature as the best representation we have of that cultural fusion. Robinson's attention to cultural interaction along the border led him to see not just that the border had been crossed but that there were people for whom the border is not a wall but a bridge. The cultures that have come into contact along the border must learn to coexist, and the respect for difference and willingness to find common ground everywhere exhibited in Robinson's work would take us a long way toward that coexistence.

I have not tried here to discuss every aspect of the essays that follow, which in any case can speak for themselves. What I have tried to do is to draw out the ways in which these essays and Robinson's other work can serve as examples. When one looks for work on the literature and culture of the Southwest and the borderlands, Cecil Robinson's work stands virtually alone in its mastery of the material and its sophistication. Yet in any attempt to achieve a more pluralistic vision of American culture, the contribution of the Southwest is essential and potentially enormous. If the task facing the United States today is to arrive at a harmonious synthesis of our received European heritage and the non-European cultures represented by our minorities and our immigrants, then the Southwest represents a crucial model and laboratory. *No Short Journeys* represents the final work of a man who studied that model with care and insight, and I think anyone interested in understanding the dynamics of multiculturalism in the Americas can learn from his work.

REED WAY DASENBROCK

# Preface

The unique aspect of the borderlands between the United States and Mexico is that they both separate and bring together two widely disparate cultures. It is somewhat awe-inspiring to consider that the moment one crosses the border into Mexico, one has taken the first step into a cultural region that extends all the way to the tip of South America. Yet though Mexico has a number of things in common with the huge Hispanic American world, including such primary things as language and religion, Mexico is one of the most distinct entities in Hispanic America. With its strong cultural personality, it radiates its influence into the American Southwest.

The essays in this book examine in different ways the cultural interplay between North America and Hispanic America, and more specifically between the United States and Mexico. The first essay, "The Fall of the 'Big House' in the Literature of the Americas" takes the macro approach in relating the two main cultural areas, whereas the subsequent essays are concerned specifically with the relations between the United States and Mexico. Even the first essay, with its wider scope, does, in its treatment of the downfall of the Mexican masters of the great estates in the Southwest as the Americans took over the area, deal with the Southwestern regional situation. I have not included in this text a treatment of the conflicts in the Southwest between Mexicans and various Indian tribes. This is a separate subject and does not properly fit within the scope of the intentions of this book.

These essays have, for the most part, been previously published in various journals and books, but they have been revised, expanded, and updated to make them suitable for this volume and for a new and wider look at the entire subject matter.

# No Short Journeys

# 1

## The Fall of the "Big House" in the Literature of the Americas

In Latin America the word *Americano,* when used in a formal sense, usually applies to the Americas as a whole, whereas clearly the word *American* in North American ears applies only to the United States. We North Americans are still considerably ethnocentric and have not yet developed the hemispheric sense. It is also true that the literatures of the United States and Latin America grew up in considerable isolation from each other, though generally Latin Americans have known more about North American literature than has been true of the reverse situation. Only in relatively recent times have North Americans interested in literature begun to be attuned to such names as Gabriel García Márquez, Mario Vargas Llosa, Carlos Fuentes, Julio Cortazar, and Manuel Puig. It is gratifying that this awareness has come into being, and yet one cannot escape the sense that to many North Americans, Latin American literature seems to have burst into being with the arrival of these authors. In fact, however, the two literatures representing the two principal cultures of the Western Hemisphere have been maturing steadily since colonial times, and for the greater part of the time have been quite unaffected by each other. Yet despite this lack of communication, there are some striking parallels. One would expect these in narratives of the discovery, conquest, and settlement of the New World, and such parallels are indeed

An earlier form of this essay appeared in *The Arizona Quarterly* 24 (Spring 1968): 23–41.

to be found. However, the North American reader venturing into the literature of Latin America might not be prepared for the "shock of recognition" that awaits. In both cultures, writers unknown to each other but experiencing similar historical and social circumstances have produced novels which, however different in "personality," have significant similarities.

There is, in particular, one area in the life of the Americas in which a parallel historical, social, and economic experience has produced a literature whose kinship is undeniable. I refer to the phenomena of the "big house" and the great plantations, of the masters and the slaves, of the splendor and hauteur of a landed aristocracy, and of its destruction by the whirlwind. This literature, which at its worst has brought forth the "moonlight and magnolia" genre of our South, has at its best a high degree of artistry and has given us the opportunity to understand at the deepest level of our perception events which bear most importantly upon our times.

Of the role played by the "big house" in Latin America, Frank Tannenbaum, historian of Latin American civilizations, writes:

> It would be no exaggeration to say that the hacienda, or as it is known in Brazil, the *fazenda,* set the tone and determined the quality of Latin American culture during the nineteenth and early part of the twentieth century. . . . The hacienda is not just an agricultural property owned by an individual. It is a society, under private auspices. The hacienda governs the life of those attached to it from the cradle to the grave, and greatly influences all the rest of the country. . . . It is also a social, political, and cultural institution."[1]

Much the same could have been said of the plantations of the antebellum South of this country. It is not surprising that an institution such as the "big house," being in fact a self-contained culture, should have produced a literature of its own. It is extensive, epical in its sweep, and finally poignant and tragic. The fall of the "big house" set the conditions for a new social reality and a new literature throughout the Americas.

In Latin America, the "big house" developed in different ways. In Argentina, Uruguay, and southern Brazil, it supervised the cattle industry and therefore had affinities with the great ranches of our West during the epoch of the great cattle kingdoms. However, these *estancias,* as they were called, were manorial in their way of life. Their *patrones* tended to be patriarchal aristocrats, passing on their rule from generation to generation. In their feudal manner of life, they resembled more the owners of the plantations of the old South in this country than they did the ranchers of our West.

In the literature of Argentina, the *estancia* tends to be the villain of the piece rather than the victim. The most remarkable literary genre of country life in Argentina is the literature of the gaucho. The tragedy of this once freewheeling horseman of the pampas was that eventually he was fenced in and reduced to the degraded status of worker and semi-serf on the *estancia*. Yet in the literature of Argentina, this nomadic cowboy stands as a symbol of defiant freedom, of refusal to bend the knee in servitude. Argentina's great writer and educator, Domingo Faustino Sarmiento, generally disapproved of the gaucho as a barbarian who stood in the way of progress and, when he turned politician, became a crude tyrant. Yet in his greatest work, *Facundo,* modeled on the career of just such a gaucho become caudillo, Sarmiento could not conceal his admiration for the gaucho in his stoic toughness, courage, and mastery of the life of the pampas. Argentina's national epic is the long poem "El gaucho Martín Fierro," written in 1872 by José Hernández. Martín Fierro is the hero of frontier individualism against the impositions of society. The gaucho genre in Argentina reached its apogee in 1926 with the appearance of the affecting, crepuscular novel *Don Segundo sombra* by Ricardo Güiraldes, in which the figure of Don Segundo, more symbol than man, glides through the book, initiating the protagonist into the gaucho ideals of incorrigible nonconformity and of free manliness. Always in the background is the "big house," the *estancia,* as threat to gaucho freedom.

In the literature of Peru, the "big house" has also been shown as the usurper of human freedom. In one of Peru's most famous novels, *El mundo es ancho y ajeno* (Broad and Alien Is the World), written by Ciro Alegría in 1941, an Indian community is annexed by a white landlord and its inhabitants reduced to serfdom, with the connivance of the law, the army, and the church.

Other writers who have treated the "big house" unsympathetically and completely from the outside are the novelists of the Mexican Revolution. Celebrating the downfall of the dictatorship of Porfirio Díaz and chronicling the "wind that swept Mexico," such writers as Mariano Azuela, Martín Luis Guzmán, Gregorio López y Fuentes, and José Rubén Romero produced in the first decades of the twentieth century pungent novels which, in their admirable realism and authentic reproduction of the speech of the people, strongly influenced the development of the modern realistic novel in the Spanish language. The "big house," when it appeared in these novels, was caught in the cataclysm of revolution and in the act of crashing to the ground.

However, in seeking similarities between the literature of the "big house" in the United States and in Latin America, one can find the closest parallels in the literatures of our South and of the Northeast of Brazil. In both areas, the great plantations flourished not only as enterprises but also as ways of life. Brazil's extraordinary sociologist and man of letters, Gilberto Freyre, has made a definite point of this similarity. Writing to his fellow countrymen about the United States, he declared that the Brazilian traveler going through the deep South could not but be struck by a sense of familiarity. He would find himself in a region

> where a patriarchal economy created almost the same type of aristocrat and of Big House, almost the same type of slave and of slave quarters, as in the north of Brazil and in certain portions of our own South; the same taste for the settee, the rocking chair, good cooking, women, horses, and gambling; a region that has suffered and preserved the scars. . . . Every student of the patriarchal regime and economy of slave-holding Brazil ought to become acquainted with the "deep South."[2]

The American Southerner, on his part, has historically felt affinities to the sugar-growing regions of Latin America, beginning in the Caribbean islands and moving southward to the great sugar plantations of Brazil. Faulkner's demonic Thomas Sutpen in the novel *Absalom, Absalom!* sought out the island of Haiti in his design to convert himself from poor white to great plantation owner, Southern style. In Haiti, Sutpen discovered

> a soil manured with black blood from two hundred years of oppression and exploitation until it sprang with an incredible paradox of peaceful greenery and crimson flowers and sugar cane . . . as if nature held a balance and kept a book and offered a recompense for the torn limbs and outraged hearts even if men did not.[3]

Some of the Caribbean writers, however, make it clear that the white masters kept no balance book, in Faulkner's sense, when it came to black slavery. In the novel *Cecilia Valdés* by the Cuban writer Cirilo Villaverde, a wealthy Creole woman, Rosa Gamboa, smugly defends her husband for profiting from the illicit slave trade in Cuba:

> And when it comes to that, far from doing anything bad or wicked, Gamboa does them a kindness, something for which he ought to be praised, because

if he receives them and sells them, savages you understand, he does it so they may be baptized and to give them a religion, which certainly they never had in their own country.[4]

But even Doña Rosa is horrified when her husband calmly tells her that the crew on a slave ship in which he had a heavy financial interest threw a number of blacks overboard to lighten the ship, which was being chased by a British vessel seeking to enforce the anti-slave trade laws:

"Angels in heaven," exclaimed Doña Rosa, unable to contain herself. "And to think that perhaps they were not baptized," she added. "In any case— those poor souls—" "Fancy believing that those sacks of coal from Africa have a soul and that they're angels. Why Rosa, that's blasphemy," interrupted her husband brusquely. "That's just how all these erroneous ideas start. One of the pretexts the English use to justify their efforts to stop the slave trade is just what you're saying."[5]

But the American Southerner knew that the Caribbean islands were only a stepping-stone to a much larger region, the continent of South America, and especially Brazil's Northeast, that great bulge which gropes toward Africa.

The only Southern expansionist dream which had imaginative depth was the notion of a Caribbean slave empire, which found its most spectacular expression in the Ostend Manifesto of 1854. . . . Southward the Caribbean led to South America, where the slave empire of Brazil offered the world's most promising theater for the expansion of the plantation system.[6]

For a while this was heady stuff for the American South, "the purple dream," as Stephen Vincent Benét called it in *John Brown's Body:*

Of the America we have not been
The tropic empire, seeking the warm sea,
The last foray of aristocracy.

The dream was powerful enough, according to Henry Nash Smith, "to inflame a young printer and newspaperman in Keokuk, Iowa, Sam Clemens by name, who set down the Mississippi in 1856 on his way to found a coca plantation on the Amazon."[7]

But after the Civil War, the South had to drop the idea of conquest in Latin America. Nevertheless, in one of the strangest episodes in American history, hundreds of Southerners, after the defeat of the Confederacy, migrated to Brazil in the hopes of reestablishing the old slaveholding plantations and the old patriarchal way of life in a land which seemed to match their own experience. The immigrants, however, soon faced disillusion. Brazil was, at that time, undergoing a profound social revolution.

> For a long time the rise of Negroes and Mulattoes had been going on, and the Southerners found themselves, to their stupefaction, in a society in which the color criterion was not the dominant one for social classification. With consternation they saw Mulattoes and Negroes in the bosom of society, occupying important positions, and, through that fact, ceasing to be regarded as Negroes.[8]

While some of the transplanted Southerners managed to achieve a degree of success, others slipped into a Brazilian counterpart of Southern crackerdom. Whatever their individual fates, their activities were a far cry from the goals of "the purple dream."

With the end of the Civil War in the United States, the culture of the "big house" in the American South faced destruction, yet the legends surrounding the life of the "big house" survived and even thrived in "the powerful and persuasive myth of the Southern plantation." As developed by post-Civil War Southern writers, "the idealized image of the plantation," wrote Smith, "proved to have a strong appeal to Northern as well as Southern audiences, and indeed to this day forms an apparently indestructible part of the national store of literary themes."[9]

In Latin America, the great plantations with their self-contained cultures survived considerably longer than did their counterparts in the American South, continuing their sway into the twentieth century. These plantations, too, spun their legends, and the result has been a Western Hemispheric literature with much in common. In the literature about the code of the "big house," it is difficult to sort out the legendary from the real; one seems to shade into the other. An example of the stereotype of the gentleman of the Southern plantation in the United States would be Colonel Dangerfield in James K. Paulding's *Westward Ho!,* an early novel reflecting the westward exodus of Virginia planters. The colonel was aristocratic, prodigal, generous to a fault, charmingly impractical, and quick to anger and resort to arms when he fancied his honor slighted. He was a lover of horses and a gambler by nature. Without too many modifications, this figure could be made to fit one of the descriptions of a Southern type in W. J. Cash's *The Mind of the South* or some of the presumably realistic portraitures in the works of George Washington Cable, William Faulkner, Allen Tate, or Katherine Anne Porter. As a result of his studies of the life and character of the *senhores do engenho,* the lords of the Brazilian sugar plantations, Gilberto Freyre, in discussing the

gentleman complex, offers descriptions which match the character of
Colonel Dangerfield quite closely.

These picturesque or somewhat ridiculous qualities, however, should
not be overemphasized. The feudal lords of the "big house" were often
quite formidable, ruling their fiefs with the easy but absolute air of
patrician authority. In North American literature, the type dates as far
back as William Byrd of colonial Virginia. Major De Spain, in Faulkner's
*The Bear,* rules his hunting party as though it were a private army, and its
members render him absolute fealty. Such powerful patriarchs are also to
be found in the literature of Latin America. A list of them would include
Don Candido Gamboa in Villaverde's *Cecilia Valdés,* Santos Luzardo in
Rómulo Gallegos's *Doña Barbara,* Dom José Paulino in the sugarcane
cycle of novels by José Lins do Rego, and Don Jerónimo de Azcoitia in
José Donoso's *El obsceno pájaro de la noche (The Obscene Bird of Night).*

The code of the "big house" as it operated in the South of the United
States is examined by the Southerner Wilbur J. Cash in *The Mind of the
South.* A marked characteristic of the code, according to Cash, was that of
personal loyalty—loyalty not to an idea, an abstract concept, perhaps not
even to a law, but to a person; the kind of loyalty, for example, that Willie
Stark exacted from his close retainers in Robert Penn Warren's *All The
King's Men.*

This kind of relationship is also characteristic of the latifundia in Latin
America. The narrator in Donoso's *Obscene Bird of Night* has derived from
his father, a poor schoolteacher, a fatuous longing for and servility toward the aristocracy in Chile. While still a boy, Humberto Peñaloza was
walking with his father along the streets of Santiago. When they passed
the stately Don Jerónimo de Azcoitia, the father "sighed . . . because of
the incurable longing that showed in his pained look and was beginning
to be my own as well."[10] Don Jerónimo is described by the author as a
man who acted out "his role of powerful land owner, of the senator who
defends the rights of his class against the claims of upstarts, of a figure
who drew all eyes to him in the drawing rooms, at the races, on the
rostrum, at the club, in the streets."[11] Humberto becomes the secretary
and retainer at the ancient family estate of Don Jerónimo. Though the
servant worships the master, he also envies him and fantasizes trading
places with the master, even in the marital bed. However, during most of
the novel he is at least overtly loyal and spends his life in the family
service. The implied irony is that this lower-middle-class Chilean man,
Humberto Peñaloza, rather than joining forces with elements shaping the
future of his country, has chosen to identify himself with the very end of

the line of a once-powerful family, thus clinging to an obsolete mode of life.

A similar quality of subjective, personal loyalty is vivified in a scene in a Brazilian novel, *Gabriela, Clove and Cinnamon,* by Jorge Amado, whose setting is the cacao plantations in Bahia. Colonel Amancio is explaining to a newcomer to the politics of the region why he, Amancio, had been supporting this man's political opponent, Colonel Ramiro.

> I stood against you because Ramiro was not just my friend, he was like a father to me. I never bothered to ask who was right. What for? If you were against him, I was against you. If he were still alive, I'd stand with him against the devil."[12]

Part of the feudal apparatus of the "big house" in the American South was its famed chivalric deference to the ladies. Much of this chivalric mode was undoubtedly inherited from England's landed gentry. However, W. J. Cash, in attempting to explain what he considers to be an exaggerated and almost obsessive idolizing of the woman of the house, theorizes that it was often an effort on the part of men to compensate for guilt feelings because of sexual alliances with black women. Such alliances were also characteristic in the plantation regions of Latin America. Though perhaps less attended by guilt feelings than in Anglo-Saxon America, miscegenation in Latin America could give rise to family complications. Cecilia Valdés, in the novel by that name, is the octoroon illegitimate daughter of a wealthy Cuban planter and businessman, Don Candido Gamboa. She is a great beauty, and one of the people she attracts is Leonardo, Don Candido's son. Therefore, much to the distress of his secretive father, the dashing and spoiled scion of the "big house" is putting himself in the situation of making love to a woman who—though he does not know it, nor does she—is his half sister.

Though there might have been some psychological differences, the planters of the American South and of Latin America had in common a strain of masculine sexual pride. In Allen Tate's novel *The Fathers,* set in Virginia, a politician accused of sexual irregularities receives a great ovation from a male audience when he declares: "Gentlemen, I did not enter this race as a gelding."[13] This masculine pride was able to assert itself autocratically in the patriarchal culture of the "big house," giving rise to a system similar to that of the medieval droit du seigneur. The slave woman was available to the lord of the house, should he demand her compliance.

Even after slavery was formally abolished, the assumptions inherent in the concept of the droit du seigneur continued to a greater or lesser extent. This system was more openly acknowledged and probably more openly practiced in Latin America than it was in the South of the United States. Nevertheless, the presence of half brothers, begotten of black women, makes for necessary and significant elements in the plots of such important novels of the American South written by Southerners as George Washington Cable's *The Grandissimes,* Mark Twain's *Pudd'nhead Wilson,* William Faulkner's *Absalom, Absalom!* and several other of his works, and Allen Tate's *The Fathers.* W. J. Cash maintains that sub rosa sexuality between white men and black women contributes a persistent undertone to the psychology of the South. The reverse situation, relations between white women and black men, is apparently seldom the case in the American South and would violate the patriarchal emphasis.

Alejo Carpentier proclaims in his novel *El siglo de las luces,* translated under the title *Explosion in a Cathedral,* that this taboo reigns throughout the Americas:

> The white man, whose aberrations in dependent territories were viewed with indulgence, lost nothing of his prestige by making love to a black woman. And if a brood of quadroon, octoroon, or mulatto children resulted, this proliferation gained him an enviable reputation as a fertile patriarch. The white woman, on the other hand, who lay with a coloured man—cases were very few and far between—was looked on with abomination. There was no worse role one could play, between the lands of the Natchez and the shores of the Mar del Plata, than that of colonial Desdemona.[14]

Illegitimate mulatto offspring, sired by fathers or sons of the "big house," people the pages of Latin American novels dealing with plantation life. This is eminently true of the sugarcane novels of the Brazilian José Lins do Rego and of the novels that deal with the Spanish-speaking Caribbean. In *Cecilia Valdés* we are introduced to a world of lower-middle-class mulattoes who, beneath a surface of affability—particularly in the presence of whites—are seething with resentment. The author of the novel, Cirilo Villaverde, leaves the reader with the impression that, even in the nineteenth century, Cuba was headed for a major convulsion.

Gilberto Freyre, in his definitive analysis of the facets of the culture of the "big house" in Brazil, *The Masters and the Slaves,* treats the subject of miscegenation in depth. Unlike his counterpart in the American South, the patriarch of the Brazilian "big house" was more likely to acknowledge the existence of his natural children and, especially on his deathbed, might have religious qualms about them. In this connection, Freyre quotes from a will made out by Jerónimo de Albuquerque from Olinda in the northeastern state of Pernambuco, in which he addresses himself to his legitimate sons: "I commend to them all their natural brothers and sisters, and in this regard let it be enough for them to know and understand that these are my children."[15]

> Concerned for the peace of his soul, Jerónimo, great sinner that he was, then beseeches "the Virgin, Our Lady, and all the male and female saints of the Court of Heaven that when my soul leaves my body, they will conduct it into the presence of Divine Majesty."[16]

Whatever its irregularities, however, the society of the "big house" was a kind of whole world in microcosm, a completed and deeply established culture. Those who lived under its aegis knew its rules, and in accepting them had a sense of functioning within an ordered world. They were not alienated. Allen Tate and other Southern writers such as John Crowe Ransom, Robert Penn Warren, and Donald Davidson, especially early in their careers, wrote eloquent apologies for the traditional agrarian and manorial life of the South. To these "fugitive" writers, as they were called after the name of their magazine, the United States beyond the borders of the South—industrialized, citified, mass-mediumized, rootless, and inhuman—was a vast, sprawling vulgarity. They retrenched, proclaimed the old order, and issued their manifesto under the assertive title *I'll Take My Stand.*

Allen Tate's novel *The Fathers* is essentially a justification in fiction of the values of this order. One of the figures in this novel sums up the character of the masters of the "big house": "Men of honor and dignity! They did a great deal of injustice but they always knew where they stood because they thought more of their code than they did of themselves."[17] Such men were also produced on the great plantations of Brazil's Northeast. One of these was the patriarch José Paulino, hero, if not protagonist, of José Lins do Rego's sugarcane cycle of novels. Autocrat and stern taskmaster, he was, nevertheless, a man who worked outside most of the day, supervising operations in the fields or at the *engenho,* the sugar mill, alongside his black field hands. His grandson, Carlos de Mello, commented upon the old man's identification with the land that he worked upon: "Sunk in the earth like a tree, he sent down roots and sent forth branches. And no one has ever heard of trees taking holidays or resting for moment."[18]

It was the lives, manners, and standards of such men, their wives, and their children, that Gilberto Freyre lovingly studied in great detail. This remarkable man, anthropologist, sociologist, and man of letters, has had a great influence upon the important group of novelists of northern Brazil: Lins do Rego, Jorge Amado, Gracialano Ramos, and Rachel de Queiros. Lins do Rego says of Freyre: "I write about him, and I speak almost of myself, so much do I feel myself to be his creation, so great was the influence that he exerted upon my poor abilities." Though a sophisticated scholar, Gilberto Freyre, in one part of his being, is as deeply attached to the land of the traditional plantations as was old José Paulino of Santa Rosa. One can imagine the deep satisfaction he felt as he wrote the dedication of his masterpiece, *The Masters and the Slaves*—"In memory of my grandparents"—and then named those venerable men and women whose lives had been at the very core of the traditional "big houses" of the state of Pernambuco.

Yet, Freyre is no reactionary. In later books such as *The Mansions and the Shanties* and *New World in the Tropics*, he gives a richly textured account of the emergence of modern Brazil and, while noting the important role they have played in bringing Brazil to the threshold of modernity, Freyre shows himself to be reconciled to the fact that the "big houses" of the sugar lords, their power, and their influence are gone. Unlike the "fugitive" group of writers of the American South—such as Tate, Ransom, and Davidson—who remained bemused by a pastoral idyll, Freyre is exhilarated by the prospects of gigantic Brazil's coming of age, with all the pain that is entailed in its wrenching itself into modernity.

Yet it is distressing to Freyre to note the wide chasm that has opened up between the shantytowns, the *favelas*, of the desperately poor blacks, who have fled the countryside for such cities as Rio de Janeiro, and the mansions of the nouveaux riches, stoutly barred from the inside and cut off from the life of the streets. Freyre reminds Brazilians that the "big house" (the *casa grande*) and the slave quarters (the *senzala*) were not cut off from each other. Deep human relationships often cut across the formal hierarchy of the *casa grande*. While eschewing any nostrums begotten of nostalgia, Freyre asks of Brazilians that in a revolutionary age they reestablish some of the human currents of an earlier time.

In his extensive writing, Freyre always has an eye out for significant comparisons that can be made between the life of Brazil and that of the United States. In *New World in the Tropics* he comments upon one of the most interesting phenomena that Brazil and the United States have in common, the fusion of South and West, the interaction of the life of the "big house" and the life of the frontier.

Just as Negro slavery and cotton and tobacco grew up together in the Old South of the United States, so Negro slavery and sugar and, later, coffee grew up together in that vast section of Brazil where the planters were the political lords. There, as in the United States, the one-crop system moved westward to newer land, carrying with it slavery and other institutions until . . . frontiersmen and planters met and developed hybrid forms of social organization.[19]

The process by which the frontier became plantation and the rough-hewn took on the livery of Southern gentility is traced by W. J. Cash in *The Mind of the South*. Cash punctures the legend that portrays the Southern planter as having been descended from an ancient, aristocratic, landed family in England, able to display an impressive family coat of arms. There were, to be sure, says Cash, some families, especially in Virginia, which fitted this description. However, a great number of the founders of families which were to become great plantation owners were, according to Cash, Scotch-Irish Presbyterians who entered regions of the South when these areas were still frontier country. Cash presents a case history, starting his story with the statement "A stout young Irishman brought his bride into the Carolina up-country about 1800."[20]

As the story continues, we are told that this man cleared a piece of land and built a two-room log cabin. A little patch of cotton was planted, and this man put his life savings of twenty dollars into buying land at fifty cents an acre.

Every day now—Sundays not excepted—when the heaven allowed and every night when the moon came, he drove the plough into the earth, with uptorn roots bruising his shanks at every step. Behind him came his wife with a hoe. In a few years the land was beginning to yield cotton—richly, for the soil was fecund with the accumulated mold of centuries."[21]

Eventually the Irishman took on slaves, and he continually expanded his landholdings. When he was forty-five, he built the "big house," imposing with its gleaming whiteness and great columns. Gradually he fashioned himself into the model of the Southern gentleman and at his death was eulogized in the local paper as "a noble specimen of the chivalry at its best."[22]

The worlds of the slaveholding South and of the frontier met in such settlements along the Mississippi River as Hannibal, Missouri, where Mark Twain grew up. Indeed, the world of *Huckleberry Finn* is an interesting combination of South and West. There is much of the rawness, violence, and exaggeration of the frontier. Yet Southern gentility in the persons of the Widow Douglas, Miss Watson, and Aunt Sally struggles to maintain an oasis in the wilderness. In more sinister ways the South finds representatives in such figures as Colonel Sherburn and the Grangerfords. In fact, the house of the Grangerfords purports to be the "big house," Southern style, but though it aims at the elegant, it achieves the garish. The journey down the river, the spine of the novel, is one in which much of the scenery has the wild splendor of the yet unravished West, but the occupants of the raft, Huck and Jim, the runaway slave, are locked in a moral crisis, the core of the book, which was possible only because Mark Twain's Missouri was under the aegis of the institutions of the South.

In the work of William Faulkner, too, frontier and plantation fuse. Thomas Sutpen of *Absalom, Absalom!,* in his obsession to become a great lord of the manor, buys land from the Chickasaw Indians in the frontier region of western Mississippi. Upon this land, the "big house" of the plantation which is to be known as Sutpen's Hundred is raised with the help of a French architect who is kept prisoner until the job is done. Though Sutpen fancies himself now to be a gentleman planter, his behavior contains much of the old frontier crudities. The picture of Sutpen by torchlight, stripped naked and full of whiskey, wrestling his giant Negro slaves and pinning their shoulders to the barn floor presents an image which is at some remove from scenes of Southern gentility in old Virginia.

As Gilberto Freyre has indicated, the culture of the "big house" and the life of the frontier also have fused in Brazil, and this fusion is reflected in the literature of Brazil's Northeast. The novels of Jorge Amado treat the rise and fall of the colonels of the cacao plantations in Amado's native state of Bahia. Those who cleared away the jungle and set down the great cacao plantations were men of rough beginnings. However, like Cash's Irishman, once their plantations were flourishing, they aspired to more than financial success. They wanted and achieved political power. Furthermore, just as the plantation owners of the deep South modeled themselves upon the aristocrats of Virginia, so did the cacao colonels, in their effort to give themselves some polish, choose as their models the traditional aristocrats of the old sugar plantations of Pernambuco.

However, in the development period of the cacao plantations, as Jorge Amado records their history, life among the cacao colonels had much in common with the days of our "wild West." In *The Violent Land,* Amado presents episodes similar to the accounts of the range wars of the American West to be found in such novels as Conrad Richter's *Sea of Grass.*

Plantations in Bahia hired private armies of assassins and made war upon each other. As Jorge Amado put it:

> The rich man of today may be the poor man of tomorrow, if another richer than he, with the aid of a lawyer, worked a clever "ouster" and succeeded in taking his land away from him. What was more, any of today's living might tomorrow be lying dead in the street, a bullet-hole in his chest. For over and above the court of justice, the prosecutor, and the citizen jury was the law of the trigger, which . . . was the court of final appeal.[23]

Just as in the United States the plantation lands of the South grade into the open country of the Western cattlemen, so in Brazil the plantations of the rich lands of the coastal littoral are backed against Brazil's famous *sertão*, the desert backlands. The novels of the *sertão* are among the most interesting works to be found in Brazilian literature. The genre began with a notable book which is not really a novel but a vividly rendered account of a historical situation, *Os sertões* by Euclides da Cunha, published in 1902 and translated into English under the title *Rebellion in the Backlands*. In this book, a group of tough and fanatical backlanders, rallying around a religious hysteric named António Conselheiro (Anthony the Counselor), holds off successive attacks by the best armies that Brazil can muster.

Just as the cattlemen of our West resisted the incursion of any other types, such as sheep raisers or farmers, so were the *sertanejos*, the cowboys of the *sertão*, jealous of their independence. They often carried on an undeclared warfare against the great plantation owners seeking to encroach. In *The Devil to Pay in the Backlands*, João Guimarães Rosa has one of his characters say: "You know, sir, the sertão is where the strong and the shrewd call the tune. God himself, when he comes here, had better come armed!"[24] The great plantation owners were resigned to appeasing the bands of *jagunços*, as the backlanders were often called, that swept down upon them.

The plantations of the United States and Brazil, whether they were on the eastern seaboard or westward, tinged with the culture of the frontier, had one thing in common: the omnipresence of the Negroes as slaves or wage workers. Without them, the plantation system could never have existed. Their lot was hard on both continents, mitigated somewhat in Latin America by the Catholic Church, which refused to regard them as less than human beings with immortal souls. Another mitigating factor in Latin America was the whole tenor of race relationships, which, according to Freyre, never did "reach that point of sharp antipathy or hatred the grating sound of which reaches our ears from all the countries that have been colonized by Anglo-Saxon Protestants. The friction here was smoothed by the lubricating oil of a deep-going miscegenation."[25] Though it must be said that such countries as Brazil are not totally free of racial prejudices, that air of untouchability, characteristic of the North, is absent in the countries of Latin America.

The portrayal of the plantation Negro of the American South in that nineteenth-century literary genre which might be termed the "moon-light and magnolia" school invariably pictured the Negro as happy, loyal, and grateful. Such works as Joel Chandler Harris's Brer Rabbit stories convinced many Northern readers that all was warmth and harmony between the races in the South. However, not all Southern writers of that period would purvey that line. Notable exceptions were George W. Cable and Mark Twain. In Cable's novel *The Grandissimes,* set in New Orleans and the plantations surrounding it, an old Negro woman, Clemence, speaks ironically of the happy Negro: "Oh . . . white folks is werry kine. Dey wants us to b'lieb we happy. Dey *wants* to b'lieb we is. W'y, you know, dey 'bleeged to b'lieb it—fo' dey own cymfut."[26] But later Clem-ence repeats the myth in a desperate but fruitless attempt to appease the white men who are about to lynch her: "You musn' b'lieb all dis-yeh nonsense 'bout insurrectionin'; all fool-nigga talk," she wheedles. "W'at we want to be insurrectionin' faw? We de happies' people in de God's worl'!"[27]

A middle-class mulatto tailor in Havana, in a scene from *Cecilia Valdés,* is much less guarded in his talk, at least when speaking to his mulatto assistant. The tailor Uribe says to young José Dolores Pimienta:

> The white people came first, and they're eating the choice cuts; we, the col-oured people came later, and we gnaw the bones. Let'm alone, my boy, and some day it will be our turn. It can't last forever like that. Copy me. Don't you see me kissing many a hand that I'd like to see chopped off?[28]

The urge toward violence in Brazil's Northeast was not always sup-pressed but, such as it was, it was never patterned along the lines of the racial antagonisms which gave rise to the lynchings in the American South. The lubrication of miscegenation to which Freyre refers was indeed a smoothing agent in terms of social relations between the races. The fact that the lords of the Brazilian plantations not only recognized their natural sons but often educated them was a social factor of prime importance in the development of Brazil. Freyre has this to say of the *cria,* the natural son.

In Brazil many a *cria* and young mulatto, illegitimate son of the master, learned to read and write sooner than the white lads, leaving them behind as he went on to higher studies. Rural traditions tell us of many cases, cases of *crias* who made their way upward, socially and economically, by making good use of the instruction that was given them, while the white youths, upon reaching maturity, were interested only in horse-racing and cock-fighting.[29]

In fact, one of the ironic aspects of the rise of the *crias,* as Freyre tells us, is that they unwittingly contributed to the downfall of the "big house" and the system that produced them. The educated *cria* clearly had to leave the plantation if he were going to make anything of himself. He was not in line to inherit any land. He therefore tended to go into the cities and work himself into the professional and managerial groups that were arising as a result of the industrializing of Brazil. It was these groups that later took over the leadership which had once belonged to the lords of the plantations.

In contrast with the success of the Brazilian *cria,* the lot of the mulatto and bastard son of the "big house" in the American South has been a melancholy one. In *The Grandissimes* we are given a situation in which Latin American and North American patterns are curiously fused. Two brothers, sons of a Louisiana Creole planter, are sent to Paris to attend the university. They are both named Honoré Grandissime, but they are half brothers, one white and the other mulatto. The fact that the illegitimate mulatto son was sent to the university is in the tradition of the Latin American "big house." When the two young men return to New Orleans, their paths diverge sharply. The white Honoré becomes the head of a great family. The other, known as Honoré, Free Man of Color, when he first returns home, so far forgets himself as to attend the famous Octoroon Ball, where the young sons of the planter aristocrats choose their octoroon mistresses. Honoré, Free Man of Color, is recognized at the ball and thrown out bodily. Octoroon mistresses are for white men only. For the rest of his life, the dark Honoré lives in a demiworld, unaccepted by the whites and contemptuous of the blacks.

In Allen Tate's *The Fathers,* George Posey, one of the principal characters, has a mulatto half brother, Yellow Jim, who is later lynched with the complicity of Posey himself. Lacy Buchan, the protagonist of the novel, says of Yellow Jim:

I think he was the best negro I ever saw; he was the most refined negro, a gentleman in every instinct. But he was a negro, and . . . white blood may have ruined poor Yellow Jim in the end. He knew what his blood was and he had many of the feelings of a white man that he could never express.[30]

The theme of the Southern planter's rejection of his mulatto son is at the core of William Faulkner's *Absalom, Absalom!* When Colonel Sutpen refuses to recognize Charles Bon, born in Haiti of a mulatto whom Sutpen had abandoned, events are set in motion which bring the "big house" at Sutpen's Hundred down in flames and destroy Sutpen's dreams of establishing a great, landed family. Ironically, the only issue of Sutpen's loins is an idiot mulatto named Jim Bond, who escapes the flaming house and disappears.

As a kind of epilogue, Shreve, the Canadian who has heard the whole epic of Sutpen's Hundred, gives his own summing up:

> Then I'll tell you. I think that in time the Jim Bonds are going to conquer the Western Hemisphere. Of course it won't be quite in our time and of course as they spread toward the poles they will bleach out again like the rabbits and birds do, so they won't show up so sharp against the snow. But it will still be Jim Bond; so in a few hundred years, I who will regard you will also have sprung from the loins of African kings.[31]

To Faulkner, passionate Southerner though he was, it was slavery which was the original sin of the South, which had put a curse upon the land, and which had brought down in ruin the great houses and great families for which he had such a deep attachment. In Brazil, perhaps because there was not that summary rejection of the dark son by the light father, the crash was not so resounding. But it did occur, as it did throughout Latin America. In Mexico and Cuba, as in the American South of the Civil War period, "the big house" was torn down in the violence of civil conflict.

But the social and economic revolution, even without the resort to arms, has overwhelmed the "big house." As Frank Tannenbaum put it:

> The hacienda system has in fact reached an impasse from which it cannot escape. . . . The hacienda has no built-in device which will allow for reform of the system, that will enable it to transform itself so as to survive and propitiate the new ways that are undermining a traditional and age-old form of social organization.[32]

In Lins do Rego's novel *Banquê*, Carlos de Mello, weakened, end-of-the-line son of a once powerful family, allows the old plantation of Santa Rosa to be taken over by an enterprising mulatto, Zé Marreira, who will incorporate it into a new industrial system of sugar refineries. The large

Snopes clan in Faulkner's novels—metallic, rootless, and unscrupulous—complete the destruction of the old families, surprising them by a
flint-hearted violation of the rules of an accepted code in which human
values were supposed to prevail over material values. One senses the
melancholy with which Gilberto Freyre must have surveyed vestiges of a
system whose traditions were bound up with his own heritage. "In
Pernambuco," he wrote, "the ruins of the big country houses . . . are still
to be seen, and it is evident that even the stables were built like fortresses.
But all this pomp has long since turned to dust."[33]

There is, however, an epilogue to the story of the "big house" in the
literature of the Americas. In some instances it survives in a phan-
tasmagoric or in a degraded state. The modern literature of the American
South is haunted by the memory of the "big house." For example,
Blanche DuBois in Tennessee Williams's *Streetcar Named Desire* is de-
pressed by a sense of dispossession. She retreats into dream sequences of
her former life on the plantation, but the reality of her life is that she is
living in a sleazy New Orleans apartment as a dependent of her sister and
brother-in-law. The authority figure in her life is no longer her patrician
father but her sister's husband, the coarse and brutal Stanley Kowalski.

Or again, the life of the masters of the "big house" is imitated by a new
breed of interlopers, who have thrust aside the hereditary owners. The
Snopes family in Faulkner's novels and stories are a case in point. And
the three Hubbard brothers in Lillian Hellman's *The Little Foxes* are men of
little education or breeding. But they carry on their commercial schemes
in plantation houses which they have taken over. One of them is married
to Birdie, the daughter of a Southern patrician, and she lives with her
husband in what had been her father's house, shunted aside and ridi-
culed for her traditional manners and ideas.

The theme of the interloper also appears in Latin American literature.
The Mexican novelist Carlos Fuentes has produced a skillfully experimental novel in *The Death of Artemio Cruz*. What the reader knows is what
goes through the mind of the dying Artemio Cruz as he rehearses his life
in flashbacks. Cruz has exploited the Mexican Revolution for his own
advantage, cleverly and treacherously changing his loyalties at propi-
tious moments. Military power is the leverage for financial gain. By
imposing political and financial pressure on one of the old landowners,
he forces this aristocrat to agree to a marriage between himself and the
man's daughter, a beautiful and proud woman who holds Artemio Cruz
in contempt. At the end of the novel we discover that Cruz was an

illegitimate child of Indian and African antecedents on his mother's side, brought up under the most deprived conditions.

Another Mexican author uses experimental literary techniques to explore a thoroughly Mexican situation. In *Pedro Párramo,* by Juan Rulfo, the narrator comes to a small village in search of his father, Pedro Párramo, whom he has never met. The inhabitants of the village exhibit a strong urge to explain their lives. Only gradually do the narrator and the reader discover that these figures are apparitions who must compulsively explain their past lives. None of them have escaped the influence of Pedro Párramo, now dead also, who expanded his power and landholdings ruthlessly, even hiring assassins to remove anyone who stood in his way.

In *The Autumn of the Patriarch,* a decayed presidential mansion acts as a kind of parody of the traditional Latin American "big house." The author, Gabriel García Márquez, begins the novel by showing us the mansion in utter shambles, with cattle wandering through the rooms, and the general, former president of the republic, lying dead upon the floor. The general, a man of obscure origins who had thrust himself into power, had run the country as though it were his own private hacienda. His death perhaps augured a new start.

The story of the "big house," vivified and made permanent in the literature of the Americas, is possibly coming to the end of its literary permutations. It is not, however, simply a record of past times to be read for historical interest. The effects brought about by the societies of the "big house" throughout the Western Hemisphere have created the important realities of our times.

# 2

## Myth Out of Mexico:
### *The Conquest in American Literature*

The peoples of post-Columbian America, North and South, have a common experience in their history: the conquest of a new world, of indigenous peoples, and of vast and often inhospitable terrain. Varying greatly according to the kinds of Europeans involved, the various Indian cultures encountered, and the many faces of nature in the Western Hemisphere, nevertheless, in an important psychological respect, the experience has been one. As such, it has needed some quintessential expression in the literature of the Americas. Among the many tales of conquest, one seems to stand alone, lofty and detached from the details of historical conquest or from the general fabric of story and lore surrounding the period of discovery and colonization. The destruction of Tenochtitlán, ancient capital of the Aztecs, by the army of Cortez is, in its charged atmosphere of triumph and pathos, the very prototype of the conquest of the New World.

In literature, the conquest of Mexico has been an important link between North and Hispanic America. North American writers, hardly less than Latin American, have felt its power and sensed its importance as a type of the New World experience. The Spaniard destroying in his rage for gold a savage, brilliant, and innocent people has served North Ameri-

An earlier form of this essay appeared in *Mexico and the Hispanic Southwest in American Literature* (Tucson: University of Arizona Press, 1977), 3–14.

can writers as an analogue for the later continental epic of the destruction of the wilderness. Although the early Spanish writers, in reporting home about the strange and marvelous city of Tenochtitlán, emphasized that its high state of development was such as to make the most sophisticated Europeans gape with wonderment, the North American writers who later took up the theme often saw fit to emphasize for their own purposes the savagery and innocence which underlay this dazzling display of civilization.

However, in order to portray the Aztecs as part of a virginal America soon to be despoiled, North American writers obsessed with this idea had to mute certain of the darker phases of Aztec life, the grisly side of its religion with its torture and human sacrifice.

Though Prescott more than any other American writer influenced American authors writing about the conquest, he gave little encouragement in *The Conquest of Mexico* to contemporary and later writers who were to present the Aztecs as a case of innocence betrayed. While not minimizing Spanish barbarities, Prescott insisted that the conquest was in the main a deliverance from the terrors of the god Huitzilopochtli to the mildness and love of the Virgin of Guadalupe. A modern writer, Frances Gillmor, who has combined creative gifts with dogged and ingenious scholarship in re-creating the lives and times of two Aztec leaders, insists that she, too, is not to be identified with the concept of the Aztec as noble savage betrayed. Her two books dealing with Aztec themes are written in the manner of biographical narrative. They are *Flute of the Smoking Mirror*,[1] a study of the poet-statesman of Texcoco, Nezahualcoyotl (1402–1472), and *The King Danced in the Market Place*,[2] a biography of Huehue Moctezuma Ilhuicamina, grandfather of the famous Moctezuma II and the leader who first made the Aztecs into a formidable power, extending their domain over neighboring peoples.

These books admirably convey to the reader the author's sense of the color and tone of Aztec society and the psychology of the people. A society and its leaders are dealt with as worthy in themselves of recording and interpretation, leaving untouched the question of innocence or betrayal. However, Frances Gillmor has verbally stated that Indianists inside of Mexico and without are guilty of distortion in underestimating the role that Spanish culture and Christian idealism have played in the development of Mexican society. George Valliant, on the other hand, in his small and classic volume, *The Aztecs of Mexico*,[3] while reporting fully on the horrors, placed them in their proper context in a complex and affecting religious symbolism ranging from the gaiety of flower festivals to the sacrificial stone and obsidian knife. He insists that with the destruction of Tenochtitlán a uniquely aesthetic vision of life perished.

A cherished myth, of course, is not to be overthrown by facts or by rationalistic analysis. Furthermore, the idea of the conquest as the destruction of innocence, which has flourished in American letters for over a century, certainly expresses *a* truth, if not the whole truth. The very imminence of total disaster has made every knowable detail of Moctezuma's city seem especially precious to novelists and poets. Brooding in the approved manner of early-nineteenth-century romanticism over the lost glories of the Aztecs, Robert Montgomery Bird, somewhat in the spirit of Whitman's "Muse in the New World," heralds the Aztecs as a source of a New World mythology for literature and theorizes that

> nature, and the memory of strange deeds of renown, have flung over the valley of Mexico a charm more romantic than is attached to many of the vales of the older world; for though historic association and the spell of poetry have consecrated the borders of Leman and the laurel groves of Tempe . . . yet does our fancy, in either, dwell upon objects which are not so much the adjuvants of romance as of sentiment; in both, we gather food rather for feeling, than imagination; we live over thoughts which are generated by memory, and our conceptions are the reproductions of experience. But poetry has added no plenary charm, history has cast no over-sufficient light on the haunts of Montezuma;[4] on the Valley of Lakes, though filled with the hum of life, the mysteries of backward years are yet brooding; and the marvels of human destiny are whispered to our ears; in the sigh of every breeze. . . . One chapter only of its history (and that how full of marvels!) has been written or preserved; the rest is blank. . . . This is the proper field for romantic musings.[5]

Two modern American poets have recited, one in prose, the other in verse, long lists of objects of commerce and art that were to be found in the ancient capital of Mexico at the time of Moctezuma. The objects are rendered almost tactile to the reader, and the naming is the poetry. In his book of essays *In The American Grain*, William Carlos Williams assesses "The Destruction of Tenochtitlán" as a significant event in the American experience. Of that city he writes:

> Here "everything which the world affords" was offered for purchase, from the personal service of laborers and porters to the last refinements of bijouterie; gold, silver, lead, brass, copper, tin; wrought and unwrought stone, bricks burnt and unburnt, timber hewn and unhewn, of different sorts; game of every variety, fowls, quails, partridges, wild ducks, parrots, pigeons, reed-birds, sparrows, eagles, hawks, owls, likewise the skins of some birds

of prey with their feathers, heads, beaks, and claws; rabbits, hares, deer and little dogs, which they raised for eating; wood and coals in abundance and braziers of earthenware for burning coals; mats of various kinds; all kinds of green vegetables, especially onions, leeks, watercresses, nasturtium, sorrel, artichokes, and golden thistle; fruits, fish, honey, grain—either whole, in the form of flour or baked into loaves; different kinds of cotton thread of all colors; jars, jugs, pots, and an endless variety of vessels, all made of fine clay, most of them glazed and painted; eggs, cakes, pates of birds and fish; wine from the maguey, finally everything that could be found throughout the whole country was sold there, each kind of merchandise in a separate street or quarter of the market assigned to it exclusively, and thus the best order was perserved.[6]

To Williams the epic of Cortez and Moctezuma was the very stuff of the "American grain." He goes on to enumerate the gifts which Moctezuma sent to Cortez in an effort to placate him and forestall his march on the capital:

. . . a gold necklace of seven pieces, set with many gems like small rubies, a hundred and eighty-three emeralds, and ten fine pearls, and hung with twenty-seven little bells of gold. Two wheels, one of gold like the sun and the other of silver with the image of the moon upon it, made of plates of those metals, twenty-eight hands in circumference, with figures of animals and other things in bas-relief, finished with great skill and ingenuity.—A headpiece of wood and gold, adorned with gems, from which hung twenty-five little bells of gold, and on it, instead of plume, a green bird with eyes, beak, and feet of gold.—Several shoes of the skin of a deer, sewed with gold thread, the soles of which were made of blue and white stones of a brilliant appearance.—A shield of wood and leather, with little bells hanging to it and covered with plates of gold, in the middle of which was cut the image of the god of war, between four heads of a lion, a tiger, an eagle and an owl, represented alive with their hair and feathers.—Twenty-four curious and beautiful shields of gold, of feathers, and very small pearls, and four of feathers and silver only.—Four fishes, two ducks and some other birds of molten gold.—A large mirror adorned with gold and many small pearls.— Miters and crowns of feathers and gold ornamented with pearls and gems.—Several large plumes of beautiful feathers, fretted with gold and small pearls.—Several fans of gold and silver mixed together; others of feathers only, of different forms and sizes.—A variety of cotton mantles, some all white, others chequered with white and black, or red, green, yellow, and blue; on the outside rough like shaggy cloth and within destitute of color and nap.—A number of underwaistcoats, handkerchiefs, counterpanes, tapestries and carpets of cotton, the workmanship superior to the materials of which they were composed.—And books made of tablets with a smooth surface for writing, which being joined might be folded together or stretched out to be a considerable length. . . .[7]

Needless to say, all these gifts, rather than deterring Cortez, roused his cupidity the more and strengthened his resolve to conquer the heart of the Aztec empire.

The other poet, Archibald MacLeish, in his narrative poem *Conquistador* speaks with the voice of Bernal Díaz del Castillo, veteran campaigner who had fought under Cortez in all the battles of the conquest. Bernal Díaz's account of the conquest, *La verdadera historia de la conquista de Nueva España (The True History of the Conquest of New Spain)*, was the source upon which Prescott relied the most. Directly, or indirectly through Prescott, it has influenced most American writers dealing with the conquest. It was written in the form of a memoir in the soldier's old age, and MacLeish catches much of the spirit of the original chronicle in its nostalgia and testiness as well as in its clarity, matter-of-factness, and eye for detail. Bernal Díaz retained a remarkable memory for the minutiae of life in Tenochtitlán as it was first seen by Cortez and his men. In *Conquistador* MacLeish has him speak of the varied commerce of the city:

Merchants of sweet nuts and of chives and of honey:
Of leaves of dock for the eyes: of a calf's bone for

Gloss of the hair as the hand draws it; of dung
For salt for the tanning of leather; sellers of yarn:
Old men with the sun-bleached hair and the bunches of

Herbs: of lettuces washed cool: of garlic
Dried brown on a withy of plaited grass:
Sellers of cooked dough by the coal-fires larding the

Stained skirt with the skittle of burning fat:
Those the makers of robes: Those that shredded the
Silken down of a seed and their fingers fashioned the

Stone to the twist of it turning the scarlet thread:
Sellers of gold dreams: of blue clay for the
Baking of gods: of quills of the gold: of hennequin

Sellers of beetles for red dyes: makers of
Stone masks of the dead and of stone mirrors:
Makers of fortunate knots: magistrates in the

Swept porch: and they kept the names of the year:
They took the tax on the red stones and the herons:
They judged the levies of salt: vendors of syrups:

Of harsh drugs for the old from the coupling of hares:
Of dry seeds: of sweet straws. . . .[8]

The contrast of elegance and barbarity arouses wonder. Pursuing his reflections in "The Destruction of Tenochtitlán," William Carlos Williams writes of Moctezuma:

> Surely no other prince has lived or will ever live, in such a state as did this American cacique. The whole waking aspirations of his people, opposed to and completing their religious sense, seemed to come off in him and in him alone: the drive upward, toward the sun and the stars. He was the very person of his ornate dreams, so delicate, so prismatically colorful, so full of tinkling sounds and rhythms, so tireless of invention. Never was such a surface lifted above the isolate blackness of such profound savagery.[9]

Another modern American writer, John Houghton Allen, in the novel *Southwest,* an original work savoring authentically of the borderlands, treats a similar theme in a strange way. He writes of the capital city of the Toltecs, predecessors of the Aztecs, and, perhaps because of his Catholic background, has a character in the novel present these people not as splendid and innocent barbarians but as victims of a fall from grace. The book, written in the first person, is mainly about the borderland between Texas and Mexico. The principal characters are Mexican rancheros and ranch hands among whom the author was raised. Loosely constructed and drawling its way from tale to tale in the manner of campfire reminiscences, the book is loaded with the lore, proverbs, and turn of speech of the borderlands, and meanders back and forth through the first decades of the twentieth century as various characters remember tales of great bandits or heroes of the revolution, such as Pancho Villa and his *dorados.* But there is an unexpected interpolation toward the end of the book, nightmarish, Poe-like in its weirdness and convincing otherworldliness. One remembers that Allen is quite consciously Southern, by way of Texas.

"We had a weird story told to us by a dope addict," writes Allen, casually getting his story under way, "around the campfire at Agua Dulce one Christmas Day. Perhaps we were the sort of men who attracted weird and violent tales, but the fact remains, if you told us a story it had to be good." The Mexicans present had celebrated their Christmas the night before in traditional style "at the posada and by going to their annual Mass." Now they were back at work on the ranch and *crudos,* that is, suffering from hangovers. "It was a pitch-dark night, and the day had been gray as a fog, with the brush twisted and tortured and bare under overcast skies." The men sitting around the fire were "passing the bottle, because of the nip in the air, and because, after all, it was Christmas," when suddenly from out in the darkness a man lurched past the rim of firelight, startling all hands. It turned out that he was a harmless and pitiable creature, known to be a smoker of marijuana, "one of those grotesques that are awry and jangled from smoking this humble weed."

After eating like a glutton and praising the cook "and that alone took a *boca-de-ora,*" he launched into his story. Once as a young man he was forced to flee into the mountains west of Torreón because of a knifing. He mounted high into practically inaccessible regions of mountain wilderness, passed over a summit, and descended into an unknown valley where he discovered the "city of the Toltecs." He sneaked, full of dread, past the huge, "hawk-nosed" sentinels, who, clothed in gorgeous raiment, stood erect and looked straight ahead as though paralyzed by some enchantment. The people in the streets were frozen still, having been suddenly caught by some spell while in the attitudes of daily living. In terror the narrator fled into the principal temple, where he found a throng of people kneeling and bowed frozen in an attitude of "mysterious penance" before a high priest upon a throne. Horrified all the more, he escaped into a side room and found himself in a seraglio of temple maidens,

> all of them remarkable in that they were blonds with golden hair that fell below their waists, and fine blue eyes like clear water, and the brave laughter that would not be heard again in the Western World. They were like Valkyries, the music of Wagner. Perhaps they had been sent as tributes to the monarchs of the Western World from the Greenland colonies a thousand years ago—for they were Vikings, and they were beautiful, the tropic sun had never touched their loveliness. There was peace about their eyes, and they were the golden thighs of Paradise. The sight of them affected me with a bitter nostalgia, and again I remember, as we all remember, what the Spanish have lost in the Western World. They were like the blue-eyed, golden-haired Spanish descended from the Visigoths, that we all in our subconscious remember. It is not that we are people dark by nature, attracted to the light, the tall, the fair; it has been with us since we first came to the Indies, that we suffered a fall from grace—for the Captains of Cortés were massive men with red beards and light hair and blue eyes and voices like Thor—and we would remember the Visigoths. We have a bitter nostalgia for

blondness, we brown little men, we yearn back to our ethos, we would dream of the fair people, with blue eyes, that even the Indians believed in—and we have remembered the Visigoths.[10]

These temple maidens were imprisoned by some spell and seemed to long for the release that a Christian benediction might have given them,

> but the very idea gave me a cold sweat, and I came away from the temple maidens and I found myself in the streets again, rushing through the streets of that awful city, the people crying havoc, for they seemed to cry after me to stop and heal them with a Christian benediction—this is what they had been waiting for for a thousand years! . . . I imagined the dismay on their faces, I dared not look at them from fear and shame, but they cried aloud, at last. There was a babble of voices for a moment, and then silence. They had waited for a Christian for a thousand years, and I ran.[11]

The theme of the failure of the European in his relations with the original people of America is still here, but the point of view is different. The Europeans did not dare bestow real Christianity upon those who desperately needed it.

Though early American novelists dealing with the conquest relied almost totally on Prescott and Bernal Díaz for their source material, they did not match either of these writers in enthusiasm for the great conquistador. In the main, the Spaniard was the despoiler, and American writers have tended to find a community of spirit with that aspect of the Mexican soul which has not permitted a statue of Cortez to be erected throughout the length and breadth of Mexico. The modern Mexican historian Wigberto Jiménez Moreno has said that the Mexican psyche still bears the scars of the trauma caused by the rape of the Indian mother by the Spanish father. A recent and rather striking revelation of how close to the surface is the intense feeling which survives in Mexico about the fate of the Aztecs was the furor caused by the discovery in the south of Mexico of the alleged bones of the last of the Aztec emperors, Cuauhtémoc (this Nahuatl name also has various spellings in English). Of a very different mettle from his uncle, Moctezuma II, Cuauhtémoc defied the Spaniards while his city was reduced to rubble, block by block, and his people subsisted on rats. He never surrendered but was captured and promised honorable treatment. Cortez brought him along on his expeditions to the south, not daring to leave him in the capital. In the course of the expedition, Cortez had Cuauhtémoc hanged, claiming that the Aztec leader was plotting treason.

In an early American novel, *The Infidel,* Robert Montgomery Bird mourns the fate of Cuauhtémoc, or Cuatimozin, as that writer names him:

> Four years after the fall of his empire, and at a distance of several hundred leagues from his native valley, he expiated upon a gibbet, a crime that existed only in the gloomy and remorseful imagination of the Conqueror. And thus, with two royal kinsmen, kings and feudatories of Anahuac, he was left to swing in the winds, and feed the vultures of a distant and desert land. He merited a higher distinction, a loftier respect, and a profounder compassion, than men will willingly accord to a barbarian and infidel.[12]

In a long and idyllic novel written a decade after Bird's, Joseph Holt Ingraham celebrates "the rise and love of the first Moctezuma, whose descendant was to lose his power, his empire, and his life, by the hands of an invader, whose coming was from the rising sun, and whose pathway was deluged with blood."[13] Published the same year as Ingraham's book was Edward Maturin's *Montezuma, the Last of the Aztecs,* which conjured up the image of a pastoral, innocent, and serene Tenochtitlán on the eve of the conquest:

> Nor had nature, in the caprice which sometimes characterizes her loveliest creations, lavished these beauties for her own solitary enjoyment, or the isolated honours of her own worship. Towns, studding the bosoms of the lakes, or bordering their margins, lent the busy and populous aspect, to this sylvan eliseum, of worshippers assembled at the great altar of nature, to pour forth their hymns of gratitude, or solemnize their simple rites in honour of her who had made their happy valley one rich panorama, of her beauties, and endowed the temporary sojourn of earth with the fadeless joys, the unwithering hues, and beatific visions of heaven! Clustered with flowers or embowered in shade, lay these cottages; their quiet inhabitants occupied in the various enjoyments afforded by their pastoral retreat: some of them engaged on their *chinampas* in rearing fruit, flowers or vegetables for the market of Tenochtitlán. Alas! little did they deem their days of happy seclusion in that valley-retreat were so rapidly drawing to a close: its smiling orchards and gardens so soon to be trampled by the iron-heel of the conqueror, or laid waste by his desolating ambition; the chrystal water of its lakes darkened and defaced by the lombard and the quiet depths of their paradise re-echoing the blast of the war-trumpet or the remorseless battle-cry, "God and St. Iago![14]

Again in *Conquistador* MacLeish depicts the Spanish soldiers recognizing that in Mexico they would forever be strangers:

We praised the trampling of sun as gilt cock;
Our hearts were singing as hammered bronze and our mouths with

Sound as the corn is where the wind goes: and we mocked the
Shape of love with our thumbs: We cried aloud of the
Great sky: of the salt rock: of the land. . . .

And nevertheless it was not so: our tongues were
Unskilled to the pulp of their fruits as the language of
Sullen stones in our mouths: we heard the sun in the
Crackle of live trees with the ears of strangers. . . .[15]

William Carlos Williams absolves Cortez of personal blame, calling him the agent of the

> spirit of malice which underlies men's lives and against which nothing offers resistance. And bitter as the thought may be that Tenochtitlán, the barbaric city, its people, its genius wherever found should have been crushed out because of the awkward names men give their emptiness, yet it was no man's fault. It was the force of the pack whom the dead drive. Cortez was neither malicious, stupid, nor blind, but a conqueror like other conquerors.[16]

Yet, of course, all was not destruction. From practically the first day Cortez and his men landed in Vera Cruz a racial fusion began which was to produce a remarkable new culture. In fact the prefiguration of the new Mexican race was the relationship between Cortez and his new mistress, Malinche, known to the Spaniards as Doña Marina. She gave him access to the Indian world, not only in its stratagems and intrigues but also in its traditions and its psychology.

Indianists in Mexico have long hated Malinche as a traitor to her people. The modern painter Siqueiros presents her in a large mural being lasciviously fondled by Cortez as she snickers at the destruction of her people, her earth-brown body making sharp contrast with the startling whiteness of the skin of the Spaniard. And yet Malinche had real grievances. The daughter of a small chieftain on the rim of Tenochtitlán, she was dispossessed of her inheritance by the connivance of her mother. Her father died while she was a child, and her mother remarried and had a son for whom she was very ambitious. If he was to inherit the chieftainship, Malinche had to be removed; so the mother sold her into slavery and staged a mock funeral to prove that she was dead. It was as a slave in the region of Vera Cruz that Cortez came upon her. While undoubtedly she paved the way for his successes, she also gave him an understanding of and respect for the indigenous cultures of Mexico.

Cortez, unlike Pizarro, although he felt impelled upon occasion to use harsh methods, had no love of cruelty per se. The histories of Mexico and Peru might be expected to have run a parallel course. In each area the Spaniards came upon highly developed and flourishing Indian civilizations, but Mexico produced a genuine fusion of races and cultures, while in Peru a Spanish oligarchy uneasily ruled from Lima a dispossessed mass of Indians whose resentment was rising to a dangerous pitch. The nature of the conquest in each area, and more particularly the characters of the conquistadores, provide a key to this situation, and Malinche deserves no little credit for the road that colonial Mexico embarked upon. In the opening lines, MacLeish in *Conquistador* presents Bernal Díaz faced with the fact of *mestizaje,* a racial mixture, in the persons of his own children:

> . . . my children
> Half-grown: sons with beards: the big one
> Breaking the small of his back in the brothel thrills
> And a girl to be married and all of them snarling at home
> With the Indian look in their eyes like a cat killing.

In her novel *Step Down Elder Brother,* Josephina Niggli considers the social situation of the state of Nuevo León and especially its capital, Monterrey, the industrial center of Mexico. Nuevo León had long prided itself on being *criollo,* that is, of pure Spanish blood though in the New World. With the industrialization of the area, mestizos (mixed-bloods) poured into the region from the south. They came as laborers, but within two or three generations, and especially after the great revolution which began in 1910 and lasted a decade, many of the mestizos became petit bourgeois and began vigorously challenging the older families. The protagonist of the novel, Domingo Vásquez de Anda, though a scion of one of the great families, has come to recognize and accept the inevitable triumph of the mestizos. He is saturated in the history of Mexico, and as he stands over a sleeping servant girl, Serafina, who has been made pregnant by his brother, and notices for the first time the Indian cast of her features, he muses upon her lineage somewhat extravagantly:

> Perhaps on Serafina's bone there was stamped the memory of Cortes's entrance to Mexico City; of Montezuma's litter with the coverlet woven from hummingbirds' feathers. In her might still remain echoes of the great poet-emperor, greatest of the Aztecans [Nezahualcoyotl], who, like David, came from the fields to sit on the throne and there compose psalms to God.[17]

Serafina's child, though rejected by its father, is to become, through Domingo's insistence, a recognized member of the family.

But apart from the partial survival of the Aztecs in the bloodline of living Mexicans, what, if anything, survives of Tenochtitlán? A number of American writers have dealt with the subterranean continuance of Indian attitudes and ritual in the religious life of modern Mexico, a subject which will be treated later; but quite aside from this consideration, several American writers, some of whom are in no way regionalists, have felt impelled to reemphasize and reinterpret the epic of Tenochtitlán as important for the self-understanding of even English-speaking America. Hart Crane ended his long poem, *The Bridge*, which had aimed at catching all of America for the imagination, with a somewhat enigmatic reference to the eagle and the serpent, the ancient insignia of the Aztecs which is reproduced on the flag of modern Mexico. Evidently Crane felt that in the summing up of his epic this cultural symbol was not to be omitted. In another poem, addressed to the stone statue of the Aztec flower god, Xochipilli, Crane challenges the reader to avail himself of that which is enduring in the life of a "dismounted people":

> . . . If you
> Drink the sun as did and does
> Xochipilli—as they who've
> Gone have done, as they
> Who've done. . . . A god of flowers in statued
> Stone . . . of love—
> If you could die, then starve, who live
> Thereafter, stronger than death smiles in flowering stone—
> You could stop time, give florescent
> Time a longer answer back (shave lightning,
> Possess in hale full the winds) of time
> A longer answer force, more enduring answer
> As they did—and have done . . .[18]

Not only in "The Destruction of Tenochtitlán" but also in other essays William Carlos Williams has returned to the theme of the Aztecs and their relationship to the American consciousness. In discussing the type of the New World man, he rejects the notion of T. S. Eliot's enervated J. Alfred Prufrock as being representative.

> Prufrock is a masterly portrait of the man just below the summit, but the type is universal; the model in his case might be Mr. J. No. The New World

is Montezuma or, since he was stoned to death in a parley, Guatemozin, who had the city of Mexico leveled over him before he was taken.[19]

As to the legacy of Tenochtitlán, Williams says:

> One is at liberty to guess what the pure American addition to world culture might have been if it had gone forward singly. But that is merely an academicism. Perhaps Tenochtitlán which Cortez destroyed held the key. That also is beside the point, except that Tenochtitlán with its curious brilliance may still legitimately be kept alive in thought not as something which *could* have been preserved but as something which was actual and was destroyed.[20]

The theme has been with us almost from the beginning of our literature; it exists in countless popular forms and has been reappraised by serious modern American writers. We have not seen the end of it, as it is enduringly a part of the matter of America.

# 3

## Flag of Illusion:
### *The Texas Revolution as a Conflict of Cultures*

Though Americans generally, and Texans especially, have been "remembering the Alamo" since 1836 and have enshrined such figures as Sam Houston, Davy Crockett, and William B. Travis as folk heroes, the people of the United States have all but forgotten the history of these Texans when they were, at least nominally, Mexicans. Yet a review of this history can be revealing, not only in deepening our comprehension of the Texas Revolution itself but also in sharpening our recognition of the cultural divisions which still engender tensions throughout the borderlands.

An investigation into the actual abuses suffered by Anglo-American Texans under Mexican rule is not sufficient in itself to explain the Texas Revolution. Other forces were at work as well. On the one hand was the unwillingness of the American colonists in Texas to make any concessions to the customs of their adopted land; on the other was an apprehension on the part of these colonists at facing a future controlled by a government whose instability seemed chronic—it had suffered four major revolutions in six years—and whose lack of respect for the law-in-the-abstract was so counter to American traditions. From the days of the earliest American settlements in Texas, conflicts in crucial areas of human behavior developed between the Anglo-Americans and the Mexi-

An earlier form of this essay appeared in *The Republic of Texas* (Palo Alto, Calif.: American West Publishing Company, 1968).

cans. From 1822 to 1835 the revolution had been slowly ripening, and the Declaration of Causes, which became the revolutionary manifesto of the Texans, was only the hastily composed and inadequate expression of a deeply felt incompatibility. It is the purpose of this discussion to examine those profound conflicts, essentially cultural in nature, which found expression throughout Texas in rising tones of two languages, until eventually all voices became lost in the sound of cannon and rifle fire.

Despite considerable intransigence on both sides, there were, during the time the revolution was germinating, some efforts on the part of both peoples toward cultural and institutional conciliation. Stephen F. Austin, the *empresario* of the largest Anglo-American settlement in Texas, was until the very eve of the revolution the leader of the moderate faction that sought to make a genuine accommodation with the rest of Mexico. Shortly after bringing his band of American settlers to the promised land along the Brazos River, Austin had discovered that he must have his grant confirmed by the central government and left for Mexico City as soon as possible. In the Mexican capital he had to wait for eight months before getting a hearing, so he spent the time acquainting himself with Mexico's culture.

A remarkable and very complex man, capable of understanding the nuances of another culture, Austin learned the Spanish language and instructed himself in the customs and traditions of Mexico. He also made the acquaintance of most of the important figures in Mexican officialdom. His tact and deference of manner made an excellent impression upon Mexican statesmen and did much for the cause of Texas. Austin's biographer, Eugene C. Barker, says of him:

> He possessed the faculty, rare in Americans of any time and in his day almost unknown, of sympathy with an alien race, and willingness and ability to adapt himself to its national mannerisms and sensibilities. There is a sense of unreality, to be sure, about a handful of western backwoodsmen waving a patchwork tricolor and shouting "vivas" for a constitution which they had not seen and could not read, but to the ceremonious mind of the Mexican there was no incongruity, and it is hardly too much to say that studied observance of such punctilio was indispensable to Austin's success.[1]

But even Austin, as will be shown later, was capable of ethnocentricity.

Conversely, the Texans were not without their advocates among Mexican rulers. At several crucial junctures, Governor Viesca of Texas and Coahuila and the regional political chief Ramón Múzquiz effectively pleaded the cause of Texas before the central government in Mexico City.

One of the most ambiguous and interesting "friends" of Texas among Mexican officials was General Manuel Mier y Terán. He had been sent to Texas by the Mexican government as the head of a boundary commission. However, his most important assignment was to report back on the doings and attitudes of the Texans, about whose motives and loyalties the Mexican government was becoming increasingly suspicious. Like Austin, Mier y Terán was a sensitive and complicated man. He appeared in the dual role of friend and advocate of Austin and, at the same time, of one of the most effective opponents of the American settlers. Mier y Terán respected the American settlers in Texas while foreseeing what their presence would mean for Mexico. He once wrote to Austin, "You and I alone understand Texas."

On the whole, however, the situation of the Anglo-Americans in Texas was not one of cultural give and take. Mexican officials increasingly wondered why the central government had ever admitted these foreigners, harsh men with a takeover manner that boded ill for continued Mexican sovereignty in Texas. The fears of these Mexicans were hardly quieted by jingoistic statements emanating from political men in the United States. Henry Clay, for example, was on record as having said:

> It was quite evident that it was in the order of Providence . . . that the whole of this continent, including Texas, was to be peopled in process of time. The question was by whose race should it be peopled? In our hands it will be peopled by freemen. . . . In the hands of others, it may become the habitation of despotism and of slaves, subject to the vile domination of the inquisition and of superstition.[2]

Clay spoke of the plains of Texas as though they had not yet been peopled, and certainly an important aspect of the situation in Texas was the scarcity of Mexicans in the region before the coming of the Americans. With the exception of a few isolated presidios, each containing no more than a handful of soldiers, the only Mexican settlements in Texas at the commencement of American colonization were those at San Antonio de Béxar (present-day San Antonio) and La Bahía, with a total population of less than four thousand. Of these, the more important was San Antonio. A contemporary account by Lieutenant José María Sánchez will suffice to show the degree of government neglect:

> Although the land is most fertile, the inhabitants do not cultivate it because of the danger of Indians which they face as soon as they separate themselves from their houses, to which these barbarians come often in the silence of the night to do damage without fear of the garrison, for when it becomes aware

of this damage, which is irreparable, it is unable to apply any other remedy than the mounting of a continual watch, because of the sad fact of a total lack of equipment, especially military, that leaves no other recourse.[3]

Clearly one of Mexico's problems in its early days of nationhood was that, with a very unsettled political situation in the capital, it was greatly overextended in terms of governmental authority and was forced to neglect the development—or even the maintenance—of its northern territories, separated as they were by great distances and intractable deserts from the troubled political heart of the nation.

The Anglo-Americans and other non-Mexican settlers poured into this vacuum. Though Austin's grant in the area of the Brazos was the first and most important one, other *empresarios* followed close behind him with large grants of land from the Mexican government. There were the colonies of DeWitt, Edwards, and Robertson, and the Irish colonies whose *empresarios* were McMullen and McGloin, with a grant extending from the ten-league coast reserve along the Nueces and the Frio toward the northwest. Their capital was, naturally, San Patricio.

With this large influx of foreign colonists, the Mexican government became uneasy, and countered by sending Mexican families into the area. Among the Mexican *empresarios* who subsequently took over grants were De León and Zavala. However, in terms of the cultural situation that developed in Texas, it is important to note that though the Anglo-Americans were aliens, they nevertheless made up a substantial majority in a large and isolated area remote from Mexican governmental control.

When the Spanish colonial government in Mexico first allowed immigrants to enter Spanish territory in order to develop the northern regions, it stipulated that all prospective immigrants should, among other things, furnish evidence that they were Roman Catholics. During the last days of Spanish colonial rule, Moses Austin, father of Stephen, made application to the colonial governor of Texas for a grant to bring American families into the region. After an initial refusal, the grant was finally made. Moses Austin represented himself as a Catholic and implied that those he intended to bring into Spanish territory were likewise Catholics. Actually, Austin was never a Catholic, although he may have thought that the verbal acknowledgment of Catholicism as the state religion amounted to the same thing. Both Lucas Alamán and José María Tornel, vigorously anti-American statesmen in the new Mexican nation, cited Austin's religious profession to support their contention that the American migration into Texas was embarked upon deceitfully and that this movement was secretly sponsored by the United States government with the aim of eventually wresting that territory from Mexican rule. However, the grant given to Moses Austin by the Spanish colonial regime was later re-affirmed by the Mexican government in the full knowledge of the back-ground of the American colonists. Yet despite this reaffirmation, the law stipulating that citizens of the country must be Roman Catholics re-mained on the books, later to become a cause of cultural and political disturbance in Texas.

In keeping with other expressions of cultural arrogance, the Anglo-American immigrants, though they had not hesitated to declare nominal allegiance to Roman Catholicism, frequently spoke of that faith as big-otry and superstition. Stephen Austin himself spoke of the Mexican devotion to Catholicism as a "fanaticism" that "reigns with a power that equally astonishes and grieves a man of good sense." Yet he constantly admonished his colonists to respect the Catholic Church, and he was always afraid that occasional Protestant services would attract the atten-tion of the Mexican authorities and result in government efforts, hitherto lacking, to enforce the religious provisions of the colonial grants. When Guerrero became president of Mexico over the united opposition of the clergy, Austin and other Texas leaders began to hope for a governmental decree of religious tolerance. However, no change in religious policy was forthcoming.

Samuel Harmon Lowerie, in studying the letters of inquiry sent to Austin by prospective immigrants to Texas, found more questions about religion than about any other topic. He concluded that, in view of the ardent evangelism sweeping the American South and West at that time, those colonists who came to Texas in spite of religious intolerance were largely indifferent and religiously atypical of the United States. But he added, significantly, that more than a few expressed confidence in even-tual religious freedom, believing that the colonists would soon be strong enough to establish an independent government.

The government of Mexico undoubtedly knew what value to put upon the profession of faith of its American subjects. But, perhaps charac-teristically, Mexican administrators were satisfied if, without too close scrutiny, they could report that the outward forms of the law were being observed. Indeed, for purposes of avoiding religious contention, they could not have sent a better man as chaplain to Texas than Father Miguel Muldoon, whose easygoing tolerance and amiable vices for some time prevented religion from becoming an urgent issue. Nevertheless, by its very prohibition, the right of free worship took on an importance disproportionate to the amount of religious feeling among the colonists, and in their Declaration of Causes for taking up arms against Mexico, the Texans placed the denial of this right high on the list.

If the religious issue was held in abeyance for some time, another issue, more deeply personal and capable of giving rise to great bitterness of feeling, showed itself from the very beginning of the colonial venture in Texas—the issue of race. One of the reasons for the steady rise in racial tensions was that neither group had occasion to become well acquainted with the other. According to Lowerie, "the number of Americans who had the opportunity to live intimately enough among the Mexicans to develop intimacy and respect . . . can almost be counted on the fingers of one hand. . . . The opportunities of the Mexicans to come to know the Americans were, if anything, more limited."[4]

Even Stephen Austin—one of the few Americans capable of intercultural communication—occasionally indulged in ethnocentric absolutes. In a letter describing his first trip to Mexico City, Austin wrote: "The people are bigoted and superstitious to an extreme. And indolence seems the order of the day." In June 1832, at a time when the situation in Texas was becoming tense, he wrote rather complacently to General Ugartechea: "Listen, if all the people of this nation had the same industry in farming, and the love of liberty and for the constitution and the laws that the people of my colony have, there would be more prosperity and fewer revolutions."[5] Though this statement might well have expressed a reality, it also expressed Austin's failure to really comprehend, sympathetically and imaginatively, the situation of the nation with which he was dealing. The Mexico of his time had just emerged from three centuries of colonial exploitation. A hundred years were yet to pass—years of agony and tumult—before Mexico would find her true personality and style.

If Austin faltered in his efforts to understand the Mexican people, what could be expected of the average Anglo-American in Texas, who knew only the Mexicans in the immediate locality and drew his ideas of the nation from these? General Mier y Terán, in the course of his inspection tour of Texas, was bothered by the poor impression that these local representatives of his country were making. He expressed his fears to the president of Mexico in a letter written from Nacogdoches in 1828:

> It would cause you the same chagrin that it has caused me to see the opinion that is held of our nation by these foreign colonists, since, with the exception of some few who have journeyed to the capital, they know no other

Mexicans than the inhabitants about here. . . . Thus I tell myself that it could not be otherwise than that from such a state of affairs should arise an antagonism between the Mexicans and foreigners, which is not the least of the smoldering fires which I have discovered.[6]

This racial antagonism did in fact work both ways. An interesting document of the time, the diary of Lieutenant José María Sánchez (*Viaje a Tejas*) reveals the reactions of a Mexican military officer who spent some time in Austin's colony. Sánchez found in the charm and friendliness of a little American girl qualities "so rare among her people." On the other hand, the coarseness and lack of manners of the richest man in the colony appeared typical to Sánchez. The American—aptly named Groce—did not condescend to invite Sánchez and his two assistants into his home for the night; they slept outside on the ground.

In general, Mexican sources described the American colonists in Texas as being cold, industrious, and aggressive. Both Alamán and Tornel attributed the loss of Texas to racial causes. They saw something inherently rapacious in the Americans and traced this predatory aspect to their northern European ancestry, drawing a parallel with the early Germanic tribes. Alamán spoke of the American "*espíritu invasor*," and Tornel, in reference to United States expansionism, wrote:

It has been neither an Alexander nor a Napoleon . . . who has inspired the proud Anglo-Saxon race in its desire, its frenzy to usurp and gain control of that which rightly belongs to its neighbors; rather it has been the nation itself which, possessed of that roving spirit that moved the barbarous hordes of a former age in a far remote north, has swept away whatever had stood in the way of its aggrandizement.[7]

Though of course neither side would agree with the other's assessment of its other's "racial" qualities, both saw racial attitudes as playing an important role in bringing about the revolt of the Texans against Mexican rule. In summing up the Texan viewpoint, Eugene C. Barker emphasized the racial aspect. "The Texans saw themselves in danger of becoming the alien subjects of a people to whom they deliberately believed themselves morally, intellectually, and politically superior," he writes. "The racial feeling, indeed, underlay and colored Texan–Mexican relations from the establishment of the first Anglo-American colony in 1821."[8]

In considering this history of mutual antipathy, one might well wonder why Mexico encouraged the entry of the Americans into its territory in the first place. One explanation lies in the fact that Moses Austin received permission to enter Texas from a Spanish colonial regime that was about to be ousted. The wealthy Creole gentlemen who hoped to replace departing Spanish bureaucrats in the most lucrative governmental posts envisioned a liberal republic that welded French revolutionary principles to American administrative structure. They felt a warmth and admiration for the United States, which had so successfully defied the mother country. And, because the policy was so very Spanish and bore the stamp of clericalism, the long exclusion of foreigners, especially non-Catholics, was lightly tossed aside by the liberal new republic.

However, the tenure of this group of liberals—who believed that the American immigrants would develop Texas for Mexico—was to be brief. The concepts of the liberals never did take hold in *criollo* Mexico. Throughout the nation's vast and decentralized territory, local administrators received the news of the new "liberal" way of life with an uncomprehending shrug and returned to the proven techniques of vice-regal rule. The Americans who came into Texas, on the other hand, brought with them a deeply rooted democratic tradition. Herein lay the basis of another conflict which was essentially cultural in its nature. The American colonist and the Mexican native soon discovered that the same words could have vastly different meanings, depending on the traditions and conditioned attitudes of those who spoke them. "Democracy," "justice," and "Christianity," thought at first to be ideals held in common, became the rallying cries of revolution because of the differing interpretations put upon them by the American colonists and their Mexican rulers in Texas.

Cases multiplied in which the political assumptions of the Texans clashed with the political practices of the Mexicans. The colonists' custom of staging political conventions in which they drew up demands and complaints to be presented directly to the central government, bypassing completely the revered chain of command, seemed to Mexican authorities to be on the borderline of treason. Though the colonists did, in fact, suffer a number of real grievances, they themselves were guilty of an intractability, an unwillingness to make any concessions to the traditions of their adopted land. Mary Austin Holley, a relative of Stephen Austin and an early traveler in Texas under Mexican rule, described a "goodly portion" of the colonists as being

> full of pretensions and overflowing with "patriotism" often the veriest "de-
> mogoguery"; accustomed at home to vent their spleen on rulers and obnox-

ious measures, they were not slow to infuse into the before contented community the spirit of resistance on the slightest provocation, until the subject
of their declamation, by exciting distrust and jealousy, became real. They
forgot the genius and habits of the Mexican people; their newness to self-
government, their jealousy of the Anglo-Americans, by regard to whose pe-
culiarities the fair fabric of Texas prosperity has hitherto been reared.[9]

Though the Texans made loud protestations in the name of freedom,
they entered into one of their most intense disputes with the Mexicans,
ironically enough, in defense of Negro slavery. The "despotic" Mexican
government never looked with favor upon the system of slavery brought
into Texas by the Anglo-Americans. To be sure, there had been a small
number of Negro slaves in the sugar-growing Gulf states of Mexico before
the coming of the American colonists, but most of these had gained their
freedom by joining the patriot forces against Spain. The liberals in the
new Mexican government saw in this de facto freedom a favorable
opportunity to abolish forever Negro slavery in the republic. The impor-
tation of slaves into Texas seemed to these liberals to be a resumption of
the outlawed slave trade.

The Mexicans, on their side, have been accused of hypocrisy in con-
demning slavery in Texas while upholding a system of peonage which
amounted to much the same thing. There may be some justice in this
charge. When the Spanish *encomienda* gave way to the Mexican hacienda, the theoretical freedom of the *acasillado*, the worker on the
landed estate, was recognized. This liberty, however, was given with one
hand and taken away with the other. The landowners soon found economic ways to bind the peon permanently to the land by devices such as
inherited debt, easily incurred and impossible of payment, and a system
of payment by token instead of money, the token being honored only at
the estate store (*tienda de raya*). Nevertheless, Mexican administrators—
themselves mostly of the wealthy, landed class and hardly advocates of
social revolution—believed that by abolishing the legal bondage of the
*encomienda* they had left the way open for the gradual improvement of
the peon's lot.

Whether or not they had been guilty of practicing a kind of de facto
slavery themselves, the Mexicans became increasingly hostile to Negro
slavery in Texas. When, in September 1829, President Guerrero issued
his emancipation proclamation, Texas was thrown into a panic. By
frantic efforts the Texans managed to get a temporary exemption. But
there is little doubt that when a plantation owner in Texas thought of the

joys of life beyond the reach of the Mexican government, it was more often in terms of the availability of Negro slave labor than in terms of the lofty democratic sentiments that he expressed to the world.

However, on other issues general American opinion would tend to side with the Texans. The function of the military in Mexico, traditionally prominent in Latin American countries, was one that deeply offended the democratic sensibilities of the Texans. The use of soldiers to collect customs duties caused particular resentment and was to become the occasion of the first resort to arms; but it must be said in defense of Mexico that the contempt among the American settlers for the tariff laws was such that they engaged in a widespread and lucrative trade in contraband. However, by another turn of the argument, it could be said that the Texans were rightfully resentful of these tariff laws, which intruded upon their economic interests and smacked of the closed economic system of colonial Spain.

Another area where Mexican and American traditions clashed was in the administration of justice. There were, to begin with, the underlying differences between the Roman law, which assumed guilt until innocence was proved, and the English common law, which operated on the reverse assumption. Beyond this consideration, the Mexican legal system had other, distinctly Latin American aspects. One was the element of *personalismo*, by which subjective attitudes sometimes overruled the abstract claims of justice. Also, there were situations in which the executive and judicial functions were united in a manner which seemed highly improper to the American colonists.

A case in point was the somewhat opéra bouffe—but nevertheless important—affair of the burro: A man named Grey bought a burro from De León, a Mexican *empresario*, paid for it, but left it with De Leon for some time. When Grey went to claim it, De León collected from him twenty-five dollars, a cow, and a calf for the expense of keeping the burro, and then refused to deliver the burro. Later Grey, by chance meeting a cart of corn driven by De León's son, took the opportunity to attach this property—corn, cart, and yoke of oxen—in order to recover the cost of the undelivered burro. By Mexican law this action was his right. However, De León complained to the political chief, Saucedo, who then ordered Austin to have the *alcalde* (mayor) of Grey's district return the property at his expense, inasmuch as he had issued the writ of attachment. The chief further directed that the *alcalde* henceforth refrain from issuing "illegal writs," especially of such a "scandalous character."

Austin's answer to Saucedo constitutes an important document in the history of culture conflict in Texas. It is couched in typically respectful terms, but before Austin had finished, he had delivered something of a lecture to the political chief:

> I find myself in an exceedingly delicate and embarrassing situation. On the one hand, duty as well as honor and inclination, urge me to obey faithfully the orders of the superior authority; on the other hand, the same considerations cause me doubt if my compliance will not amount to an injustice, or produce fatal consequences. . . . The difficulty lies in the disorganizing principle which may be created, and also, in the belief that cannot fail to exist in the minds of the settlers, that the executive or political officers unite in their person all the executive and military, political and judiciary powers that were formerly vested in the Governors and the Spanish government.[10]

Unfortunately there is no record of the final disposition of this case, but what is known of it provides a good example of personal rule above the law. Saucedo based his judgment on the alleged affront to a Mexican official's dignity by an Anglo-American, not on the facts of the case or on the provisions of the law. Also, the affair demonstrates the confusion of the executive and judicial powers, for Saucedo had no authority to interpose in a matter theoretically beyond his jurisdiction.

Mexican authorities began to recognize the intense charge of feeling that lay behind the Texans' defense of their own political and institutional traditions. Mier y Terán observed that the American immigrants "travel with their political constitution in their pockets, demanding the privileges, authorities, and officers, which such a constitution guarantees." José María Tornel berated the Mexican liberals for having sought to copy American political principles and for having opened the door to the aggressive foreigners from the north:

> Too late have we come to know the restless and enterprising neighbor who sets himself up as our mentor, holding up his institutions for us to copy them, institutions which transplanted to our soil could not but produce constant anarchy, and which, by draining our resources, perverting our character, and weakening our vigor, have left us powerless against the attacks and the invasions of this modern Rome.[11]

Though the Declaration of Causes, hastily drawn up by the Texans on the eve of their revolt against Mexican rule, contains a number of references to specific political and economic conditions that were considered to be abuses of authority on the part of Mexico, unquestionably there lay behind this document the deep disquiet felt by the Texan colonists because of profound frustrations of an essentially cultural nature—frustrations they would have found difficult to articulate. During this period the Anglo-Americans and the native Mexicans in Texas, both proud peoples, functioned under basically different assumptions in essential areas of human behavior. Given the added combustion of race antagonism, could the results have been other than the Texas Revolution?

# 4

## Legend of Destiny:
### *The American Southwest in the Novels of Harvey Fergusson*

The trouble with the bulk of Western writing, Harvey Fergusson once observed, was that it was "sired by Sir Walter Scott and damned by the genteel tradition." In a considerable body of work, consisting of novels and cultural histories, Harvey Fergusson has set out to rectify the deficiencies in the literary record of the West that he clearly recognized. Yet his work has not received the national or regional attention it deserves. In accounting for this neglect, we cannot simply resort to blaming the "Eastern literary establishment." Fergusson has not received much support from where he might have expected it: the literary circles of his own Southwest. Perhaps his sophisticated and quite ungenteel approach to his subject matter has run counter to some provincial tastes. Furthermore, having years ago abandoned his native New Mexico to live out his days in California, he did not attend to the mutual back-scratching by which the close circle of Southwestern writers have promoted each other's works.

Despite Fergusson's definite contribution, there still remains something of a mystery as to why the Southwest, with all the stimulating aspects of its cross-cultural situation, has yet to produce a body of literature of truly major proportions. The American West, for example, has not

An earlier form of this essay appeared in *The American West* 4 (November 1967): 16–18, 67–70.

yet equaled the performance of its Latin American counterpart, the Northeast of Brazil, where a very similar frontier and "cowboy" culture has existed. The modern *nordeste* novels of Brazil have paced the literary development of their country, using situations and themes very similar to those employed by our Western writers. The works of Euclides da Cunha, Jorge Amado, Lins do Rego, Gracialano Ramos, and João Guimarães Rosa have been translated into English, some of them quite recently. They should be read with attention by the writers of the American West. Guimarães Rosa, for example, in a work translated under the title *The Devil to Pay in the Backlands,* has produced a "cowboy" novel of considerable subtlety, employing the "inscape" techniques of the literary advantgarde. While Harvey Fergusson does not command a literary style of the intricacy and resourcefulness of that of Guimarães Rosa, he does, nevertheless, write a clear and virile prose, and he displays a shrewd understanding of the macrocosm of social change and the microcosm of individual human motivation. Furthermore, he is capable of a very sensitive rendering of the "feel of place" and can report, exactly and movingly, upon the natural phenomena of the West.

Born in 1890 in Albuquerque, New Mexico (he died in 1971), Harvey Fergusson satisfied Allen Tate's prime requisite for a regional writer: he was a native. The situation of his boyhood allowed him the freedom to develop his gifts. He was able to satisfy his need for solitary experience by taking long rides on horseback into what was then still a wilderness, often absenting himself from home for days. In early manhood he turned an attentiveness that had been shaped by the minute observation of the processes of nature to the processes of human society. He came to understand that he lived in a region which was just completing an episode of traumatic change and in which the wounds were still fresh. In his autobiography *Home in the West,* he wrote: "The country as a whole was a living museum of its own history. . . . The history of my own region became as real to me as my own experience."

The press of the Southwest's tumultuous history crowding upon his own life imparted to Fergusson's records of the region's past a flush of actuality. His novels are not "historical novels" in the Walter Scott tradition. They have a toughness and kinesthetic quality that puts them more in the tradition of Dreiser's Chicago novels. Fergusson's characters are not, in truth, developed in depth as highly individualized personalities. However, legendary and somewhat mythic characters are very much in the tradition of American fiction. One does not expect to meet Captain Ahab in the neighborhood tavern. Yet the character typing in Fergusson's novels is in the direction of intensification, and does not rob the figures in his landscape of the sense of reality.

A central theme in the novels is that of racial conflict, which provides the principal motif for a trilogy later assembled in one volume, *Followers of the Sun.* The novels in the trilogy are arranged chronologically by period rather than by date of publication. The first part of *Followers of the Sun* is the novel *Wolfsong,* which deals with the mountain men in New Mexico: the first Anglo-Americans to become acquainted with the region, and men who almost universally treated the Mexicans with a towering disdain. *In Those Days,* the second part of the trilogy, is a novel which, in covering the adult life of its central figure, Robert Jayson, pioneer trader and businessman, recounts the swift conquest of New Mexico by the Americans and the consequent destruction of the wealth and traditional way of life of the old Mexican landholding families of the Rio Grande Valley. The last part, *The Blood of the Conquerors* (actually the first written of the three novels), shows the old Mexican families of the Albuquerque region in full decay and in the final stage of what was to become an almost total dispossession. The protagonist of this novel, Ramón Delcasar, a young Mexican-American who is last in the line of a once proud and powerful family, attempts to reverse the tide and compete with the gringos on their own ground. He is successful for a while. His motive in struggling against the fate that has overtaken his people is not the usual competitive profit urge of the gringo but the desire to make himself acceptable to an Anglo-American girl. When the girl's family moves east in order to prevent her marriage with a Mexican, Ramón Delcasar loses the will to fight and quickly lapses into the apathetic condition of the rest of his people.

In presenting the character of Ramón Delcasar, Fergusson reveals his comprehension of the ambiguities of the relations between Mexicans and Anglo-Americans in the Southwest. As the following passage indicates, even the aristocratic Mexican families moved in a very uncertain social environment after the Anglo-Americans had established their ascendency. Of Delcasar he writes:

> Whenever he felt sure of his social footing, his attitude toward women was bold and assured. But his social footing was a peculiarly uncertain thing for the reason that he was a Mexican. This meant that he faced in every social contact the possibility of a more or less covert prejudice against his blood, and that he faced it with an unduly proud and sensitive spirit concealed beneath a manner of aristocratic indifference. In the little Southwestern town where he had lived all his life . . . his social position was ostensibly the

highest. He was spoken of as belonging to an old and prominent family. Yet
he knew of mothers who carefully guarded their daughters from the peril of
falling in love with him.[1]

Fergusson pursues the subject of the fall of the old Mexican order in *Rio
Grande* (1933), an authoritative and highly readable social and cultural
history of the Rio Grande Valley. In two of his later novels, *Grant of
Kingdom* (1950) and *The Conquest of Don Pedro* (1954), he deals with an
intermediate era in which, in some cases, there were fruitful alliances
between the Mexican aristocrats and the incoming Anglos.

In dealing with the racial situation in the Southwest and with other
themes, Fergusson has revealed an interesting aspect of the social and
cultural history of the region that has often been overlooked. Much of the
drama of its social history in the second half of the nineteenth century is
strikingly similar to more celebrated episodes in the history of the American South, the poignancy of which has provided the occasion for the
work of some of the most gifted and interesting modern American writers. Like the South, the Southwest saw the destruction of a landed
aristocracy, but with the added problem of differences of race and culture.
The incoming gringo business entrepreneurs, before whose conniving
ways the Mexican aristocrats were helpless, are roughly similar to the
famous Snopes clan of Faulkner's trilogy.

There are also less obvious similarities. The relationship between the
*patrones* of the great Mexican haciendas of the lower Rio Grande Valley
and the poor Mexican landholders of the mountains of the Río Arriba in
northern New Mexico was very similar to the relationship of the great
plantation owners of the southern seaboard and the poor white farmers
of the backcountry. While the planter-aristocrats of the southern seaboard were generally Episcopalians, the mountain people of the South
often belonged to "way-out" sects of Protestantism, characterized by
evangelistic hysteria. In the Rio Grande Valley, the great *patrones* were
orthodox Roman Catholics, while the mountain people of the Río Arriba
belonged to a flagellating sect called the *penitentes*. In Fergusson's *Grant of
Kingdom*, Daniel Laird, a wandering preacher originally from the mountain country of the South, escapes persecution at the hands of the sup-
porters of a rich and usurping American entrepreneur by fleeing to the
mountain strongholds of the Mexicans of the Río Arriba. Despite his
racial background, he is welcomed by the poor mountain Mexicans, who
recognize that in important ways he is one of their own. Of the writers of
the Southwest, Paul Horgan and Harvey Fergusson have been those with

the technique and comprehension best suited to reveal the drama inherent in the social conflicts of the region.

In his attitudes toward the interacting social forces that produced the modern Southwest, Fergusson shows a characteristic complexity. He sympathizes with the underdog and takes a "progressive" view in social and political matters. Nevertheless, he is capable of considerable empathy with people and customs of which, in the purely rational aspect of his being, he does not approve. Commenting in the novel *Grant of Kingdom* upon an aristocratic Mexican woman, Fergusson writes: "I am no believer in the value of the aristocratic tradition. But generations of security and assured social status do give some men, and even more, some women, an almost perfect manner, and the Doña was a striking example of the fact." In the same novel, Fergusson gives his overt sympathies to the itinerant preacher, Daniel Laird, who ends his days as a radical member of the New Mexico state legislature and a fervent supporter of William Jennings Bryan and the Populists. But the legendary hero of the novel is Jean Ballard, an admittedly archaic type, who exercises an absolute though benevolent despotism over a large Spanish land grant that he has inherited from his Mexican father-in-law.

In fact, Fergusson's writing represents the paradox in the tradition of Western literature that Henry Nash Smith noted in *Virgin Land*. The solitary "romantic" figure, in love with the wilderness, avoiding towns or small communities as centers of contagion, is a type developed by Cooper and popularized by any number of Western writers. As Smith points out, those who developed the legend of Daniel Boone saw him first in this romantic light. However, almost simultaneously, Boone was being publicized as the advance guard of the forces of civilization, the agent who was to open paths in the wilderness to make way for the cities that were to stretch from coast to coast. The two images were contradictory, and the writers of the Boone legend were never able to resolve the conflict. Often, as Smith has shown us, writers have sided with one or the other vision of the West. Heroes have either been later versions of Natty Bumppo or fearless fighters for law and order. Fergusson, however, like the writers of the Boone legend, shows both strains in his work.

In his own way, Fergusson is a believer in Manifest Destiny, not as an ideal but as an inexorable process. In his novels, he frequently uses the word "destiny," but the stories he tells amount to a wry view of that concept. His most memorable characters, in fact, are figures who, combining elements of the old order and the new, momentarily arrest the forces of "destiny" and make a legend for themselves. The respective protagonists of *Grant of Kingdom* and *The Conquest of Don Pedro*, Jean Ballard and Leo Mendes, are solitary figures—loners. Leo Mendes represents the figure of the Jew as western pioneer. He leaves New York to begin life again as a traveling peddler in New Mexico, in the years before the railroad reached Santa Fe. In the small community of San Pedro he establishes a store, to the great displeasure of the local *patrón*, Don Augustín, who resents the encroachment of a gringo upon a domain that he and his family have ruled for generations. Leo holds his ground, flourishes, and eventually becomes the dominant figure in the era. Through his marriage to the niece of Don Augustín, he gains entrance into Mexican society and takes on a number of the ways of the Mexican gentleman. His house becomes a great meeting place for Anglos and Mexicans. In time Leo comes to represent a kind of catalytic agent between the two societies.

Jean Ballard, the dominant figure in *Grant of Kingdom*, first appears as a seemingly typical mountain man, a man used to spending great stretches of time trapping beaver alone in the wilderness. However, there is another component to his personality. Though his father was Virginia Scotch-Irish and typical of the stock that pushed west to be converted into those fiercely anarchical figures, the mountain men, his mother was a French Catholic from the French-settled city of Vincennes in Indiana Territory. Of her, Fergusson comments: "Despite the fact that she had grown up in a wild country, she was a wholly civilized woman, for the French carried civilization wherever they went." As a result of his two heritages, Jean Ballard carries within himself not only the impulse toward freedom and solitude but also the urge toward construction, order, and community. He represents, perhaps, an attempt on the part of the author to resolve the two strains in Western writing that Henry Nash Smith explored, both of which had their attractions for Fergusson.

Jean Ballard first feels the stirrings of a desire to settle down when he meets the beautiful Consuelo Coronel, daughter of a wealthy Mexican *patrón*. However, Ballard soon discovers that it is anything but easy to gain acceptance by members of the haughty Coronel family. In recounting Ballard's travail, Fergusson describes a way of life:

> For the first time in his life he felt the massive, inert resistance of old established things, of a people fortified by wealth, and custom, and tradition, by a way of life stronger than they were, a social pattern which was a power in itself. They did not hate him as a person, but they hated anything alien.
> Family was everything to them. Their whole society was a great family, and it was organized to repel intrusion. They did not have to insult him or reject

him or even close a door to him. They could freeze him out and wait him out. He might come and sip chocolate for months and even for years and never pass any of the barriers of custom and manner that were set up against him.[2]

Ballard, however, is no ordinary man; he finally prevails against the formidable tactics of the Coronel family—but only through the active connivance of Consuelo herself. Despite the powerful and almost omnipresent force of Mexican chaperonage, Consuelo contrives to get herself pregnant by Ballard. After the marriage, Don Tranquilino Coronel, Ballard's father-in-law, deeds to his son-in-law a great tract of land in the wilderness of Colorado that had belonged to the Coronels for generations as a Spanish grant. (Fergusson derived his conception for this grant, incidentally, from the Maxwell grant, one of the most famous tracts in the West.)

In deeding over this property to Ballard, Don Tranquilino thinks he is making an empty gesture, for the remoteness and wildness of the area is such that none of his family had ever intended to develop it. Ballard, however, immediately considers the situation an act of destiny. Equipped with his long training and experience as a mountain man, he goes alone into the wilderness of southern Colorado, makes his peace with the Ute Indians (whose language he had learned through former trading experience), and looks over the vast area that has become his. He builds a great house, develops a large ranch, and allows other ranchers and sheepherders to settle on the grant, which he rules autocratically, but fairly, while Consuelo presides over it all in the style of a great lady. At its height, the Ballard grant becomes a social and commercial center.

> The evening meal at the house of Ballard was always a social event. Seldom did less than twenty men sit down to the great table. Sometimes there were nearly a hundred, and those of minor importance had to wait for a second serving. A truly astonishing variety of human beings passed through that great dining room, for almost everyone who crossed the plains stopped at the Ballard grant.[3]

However, another form of destiny overtakes the Ballard grant. Ballard overextends himself financially and eventually is forced to sell to a cunning entrepreneur, Major Blore. This man, like Faulkner's Snopeses, was originally a Southerner, but not an aristocrat. Blore, through extensive bribery, contrives to get a fraudulent survey made of the grant. This results in the eviction of many of Ballard's long-time retainers. The last stage of the area's manifest destiny is subdivision into workaday plots

expressive of utility and unheroic living. As Fergusson puts it: "A great
gust of passion and energy had struck this place and blown itself out and
left in its wake the ruin of a proud house and a legend in the memories of
aging men."

In this novel there are the counterimages of the primitive and legendary builder, and of man the despoiler. Daniel Laird, who had been
Ballard's chief steward, escapes into the mountains after the decline of
Ballard's community. From these heights, "for the last time he could see
the town, miles away and three thousand feet below him. From where
he sat it looked incredibly small and insignificant, a minor blemish on the
face of the earth." Fergusson expresses his radical discontent when he
writes:

> Men such as Ballard, who conquered the West, were reckless men with a
> touch of the heroic about them. . . . But money is never reckless and never
> heroic. Money is cunning, and it finds and uses and creates cunning men.
> Money has a long arm. It may kill but it seldom faces its victim.[4]

As something of an epilogue he adds, through one of Ballard's support-
ers: "I had always loved the mountains and I took pleasure in the fact
that their massive resistance had saved something from the sweep of
human greed."

Thus the final note in *Grant of Kingdom*, one of the last and most
effectively rendered of Fergusson's novels, is that leitmotif, long heard in
Western literature, of the love of solitude and wilderness, and of aversion
to human centers as sources of contagion. By combining social realism
with the aura of the legendary, Harvey Fergusson achieves his most
telling effects. In the best of his novels, he vitalizes that stage in the
history of "manifest destiny" when its advance guard first broke into the
Southwest. Here were men with a sweep of the heroic to their style—and
Harvey Fergusson has given them their legend.

# 5

## The Mexican Presence in the
## American Southwest

The American Southwest, despite the advance of the pale cast of American standardization, still retains something of the vivid pigmentation which has long characterized the region. To the extent that this is so, a good deal of the credit belongs to the long-time inhabitants of the area, the people of Mexican descent.

Perhaps, before it is too late, the general American public, and particularly the Anglo-American population of the Southwest, should recognize an important debt to Mexican culture. American literature has taken cognizance of this debt for some time. Walt Whitman, who sensed that the future of American culture lay in a rich synthesis of various national and ethnic strains, saw the Hispanic Southwest as making an important contribution to this amalgamation:

> To that composite American identity of the future, Spanish character will supply some of the most needed parts. No stock shows a grander historic retrospect—grander in religiousness and loyalty, or for patriotism, courage, decorum, gravity, and honor. . . . As to the Spanish stock of our Southwest, it is certain to me that we do not begin to appreciate the splendor and sterling value of its race element. Who knows but that element, like the course of some subterranean river, dipping invisibly for a hundred or two years, is now to emerge in broadest flow and permanent action?[1]

An earlier form of this essay appeared in *The American West* 3 (Spring 1966): 6–15, 95.

Generally speaking, it is still true that we have not begun to appreciate the contribution that Mexican culture can make to American civilization. In the Southwest, cities which some forty years ago were small and savorful are now burgeoning. The new growth is principally in the pattern of Main Street, U.S.A. While recent arrivals to these cities from the East or the Middle West hurry about their business, the Mexican-American, whose ancestors gave these cities their names and their original tone, is becoming increasingly the "invisible man" in the same sense that the novelist Ralph Ellison used the term to refer to his own people, the many African-Americans of the big cities who are present but not really "seen." The imagination of poets or novelists often recognizes possibilities before the more literal formulators of ideas come upon them. If there still remain solutions and opportunities which might allow our Southwest to fulfill its cultural potentialities, it is the literary men and women to whom we should look for guidance. They have pictured the Southwest directly as they have seen it, and they have also given us a vision. Walt Whitman may yet prove to have been prophetic.

The concept of a vital synthesis in the Southwest of Hispanic and Saxon elements, propounded by Whitman, has had its literary descendants. In the late nineteenth century, a Connecticut newspaperman, Charles F. Lummis, went to the Southwest and experienced an ecstatic conversion to the Mexican culture that he found there. In a series of books with such titles as *Flowers of Our Lost Romance* and *Land of Poco Tiempo* he upbraided Yankee historians for their ethnocentric view of American history and said that he hoped to live to see a book whose author "would realize that the history of this wonderful country is not limited to a narrow strip on the Atlantic seaboard, but that it began in the great Southwest." "Why," sputtered Lummis, "there is not even one history which gives the correct date for the founding of Santa Fe, which was a Spanish city more than a decade before the landing at Plymouth Rock!"

Following a similar "road to Damascus" was Mary Austin, who left a provincial community in the Middle West to discover the ancient and richly ceremonial cultures of the Indians and Mexicans of the Southwest. After a preliminary experience in a California which was as yet unspoiled, she settled in Santa Fe, where she devoted her life to publicizing the indigenous cultures of the Southwest. She predicted—perhaps because she so strongly willed it so—a cultural fusion between Indian, Mexican, and Anglo-American which would produce a new society combining elements of grace and strength. In *The Land of Journey's Ending* she wrote:

> Three strains of comparative purity lie here in absorbing contact, the Indian, the Hispanic, and the so-called Nordic American . . . so that in New Mexico and Arizona we approach nearest, in the New World, to the cultural beginnings which produced the glory that was Greece, the energetic blond engrafture on a dark, earth-nurtured race, in a land whose beauty takes the breath like pain.[2]

Charles F. Lummis and Mary Austin, despite hortatory styles which now seem rather naive, were serious, creative, and suggestive visionaries about the possibilities of the Southwest. Some other newcomers to the scene were content to exploit, for an avid reading public back east, the merely picturesque in the Hispanic Southwest. The flamboyant Joaquin Miller celebrated "glorious, gory Mexico" in his poems, while Bret Harte peopled his San Francisco with "Spanish Californian hidalgos," full of "quaint custom, speech, and dress" and mouthing "the proverbs of Sancho Panza." In *Roughing It,* Mark Twain praised the "wild, free magnificent horsemanship" of the "picturesquely clad Mexicans." Others who worked this vein profitably were Charles Warren Stoddard, Frederic Remington, and Hamlin Garland. These writers, at least in their handling of Southwestern material, tended to be superficial popularizers. However, their point was not entirely amiss. They recognized in the Mexican an element of dash and style which gave a lift to the Southwestern scene.

Starting innocently enough, the romanticizing of "Spanish" aspects of the Southwest eventually produced attitudes which had serious social consequences, especially in California, which forged what has come to be known as the "California myth." The tone was set by such books as Helen Hunt Jackson's *Ramona* and Gertrude Atherton's *The Splendid Idle Forties.* "Spanish" Californians were pictured as elegant, aristocratic representatives of an Old World tradition. When, in the twentieth century, immigrants from Mexico began to pour into California looking for any work that they could find, their ragged appearance was in sharp contrast with the images that the purveyors of the romantic tradition had conjured up. It was decided that the old California families were Spanish, not really Mexican. Therefore, their tradition could continue to be honored (and exploited) while people set about erecting barriers against the unwanted newcomers. The distinction between "Spanish" and "Mexican" proved serviceable. Anyone with a Spanish name who had been around for some time, spoke good English, and had some money could be declared a "member of one of the old Spanish families" and could be accepted socially. As for the Mexicans, they were clearly an inferior breed.

Several contemporary writers have undertaken to expose the "phoniness" of the California myth and the distinction it has made between the original "Spanish" families and the present-day garden variety of Mexican. Two writers in particular have gone about this task with considerable relish, and in doing so they have produced work which transcends the level of the sociological tract and contributes honorably to the genre of protest writing in American literature. Ruth Tuck in *Not with the Fist* draws upon population figures to dismiss the case for aristocratic Spanish purity on the part of the early settlers in the Southwest.

> By the time the colonization of the northern provinces began in earnest, racial and cultural fusion had been going on in Mexico for some three hundred years. It has been estimated that no more than 300,000 Spaniards ever came to Mexico and that most of them were men. The indigenous population of Mexico City alone was 300,000, and it was a small part of the total Indian population. The most robust Castillian gene, in such a situation, could hardly be expected to survive, unchanged, to populate Texas, New Mexico, Arizona, and California with descendants of "pure Spanish ancestry." But such is the fiction the romantic tradition likes to maintain.[3]

The California myth suffers also at the hands of Carey McWilliams. In *North from Mexico,* he examines the backgrounds of the revered "Spanish" founding fathers of Los Angeles and their families. After naming the families and mentioning their various racial combinations, he sums up the situation:

> Thus of the original settlers of Our Lady Queen of Angels, their wives included, two were Spanish; one mestizo; two were Negroes; eight were mulattoes; and nine were Indians. None of this would really matter except that the churches in Los Angeles hold fiestas rather than bazaars and that the Mexicans are still not accepted as a part of the community. When one examines how deeply this fantasy heritage has permeated the social and cultural life of the borderlands, the dichotomy begins to assume the proportion of a schizophrenic mania.[4]

Yet certainly not the most "romantic" of writers on Southwestern themes had ever intended that their work be used as justification for contemptuous attitudes toward ordinary Mexican-Americans in the borderlands. Near the middle of the twentieth century, writers dealing with the Southwest sought to repair the damage by adopting a new realism and also by developing an interest in the historical realities of the Mexican presence within the borders of the United States. Why, they asked themselves, had Mexican culture suffered such a defeat in the area? What had happened to the splendid forecasts of cultural synthesis propounded by such writers as Charles F. Lummis and Mary Austin? Ironically, the most "romantic" of the earlier writers had touched upon a most poignant theme without recognizing its real significance. In pursuit of local color, these writers appropriated the trappings and customs of the aristocratic "big house" of the feudal Mexican families who had ruled in the Southwest before the advent of the Americans. Indeed, part of the tinge of romantic nostalgia that these writers put into their stories was achieved by giving their readers the sense that the way of life of the Mexican big house was an evanescent splendor about to disappear. However, this theme was usually treated purely for its dramatic effect, with little attempt to really examine its significance in terms of the realities of Southwestern society.

An exception among the earlier writers was Bret Harte. Despite his usually gaudy treatment of Hispanic themes, he wrote occasional pieces which displayed a keen recognition of what was happening as two very different cultures confronted each other in the Southwest. One of his stories, "The Passing of Enriquez," catches the essence of the tragedy of the fall of the Mexican "big house." Enriquez is the last survivor of an ancient Californian family. When a silver mine is discovered upon his large estate, he enters into partnership with American entrepreneurs to develop it. When it is discovered that the mine is not all that it was thought to be, Enriquez refuses to go along with his partners in a plan to mislead potential investors. When his partners recognize that he will not cooperate, they succeed in defrauding him of his lands.

Later writers took up this theme of the dispossession of the former masters and treated it effectively within the context of historical developments in the Southwest. In particular, two contemporary writers have handled this theme with literary skill and historical accuracy. Harvey Fergusson and Paul Horgan have dramatized the history of cultural contact, and sometimes conflict, between Mexicans and Anglo-Americans in the Southwest. As noted above, Fergusson, in the trilogy of novels contained in *Followers of the Sun*, tells the story of the Mexican "big house" in the Southwest, its imposing grandeur before the American occupation, and its sudden decline and fall when faced with the new order. A memorable character in the second novel of the trilogy, *In Those*

*Days*, is Diego Aragón, a New Mexican gallant of one of the old families, horseman extraordinary and self-possessed inheritor of a feudal and aristocratic tradition. In the early part of the book, he has all his extensive land intact, leisure to pursue a life of hard riding and intricate amours, and no worries. However, with the encroachment of the "gringos," the building of the railroads, and the development of Albuquerque as a strong Anglo-American business center, he feels the pressure increasingly. Little by little he sells his lands to maintain an aristocratic, noncommercial way of life. The end of the book finds him completely alone in the ruined family house, stripped of all lands. Fergusson generalizes on the subject of Diego's plight:

> And Diego was not alone in his ruin. Almost all of the Mexican families had lost their money and land, had fallen to pieces just as their great houses had done. . . . With their wide lands about them, their great storerooms full of wheat and grain, their troops of servants and their prolific women, they had seemed as safe and permanent as anything man could build. But the railroad wiped them out. The Mexicans were no good at business and couldn't make money enough to keep them up. The hands of slaves had built them and kept them intact by incessant plastering. When they were deserted their mighty walls melted in the rain like sugar.[5]

Sometimes added to the improvidence of the Mexican landowners was the connivance of cunning Anglos out to seize lands from their Mexican owners. Such was the case in the last novel of Fergusson's trilogy, *Blood of the Conquerors*. A Mexican gentleman is being systematically fleeced by an unscrupulous Anglo partner while his nephew, Ramon Delcasar, protagonist of the novel, helplessly watches his inheritance disappear. Another instance of the ruin of a Mexican aristocrat at the hand of the gringos is to be found in Paul Horgan's *The Return of the Weed*. Don Elizario's estate had been rapidly shrinking. The Don "knew it was true, and that it was a pity, that he simply wasn't smart enough to hold his money against these newcomers, these exhausting gringos. A gentleman didn't have to be smart about money, this he knew also. They got it all, of course. He saw it go, he watched their operations with a helpless affability."[6]

The story of the fall of the Mexican "big house" in the American Southwest, as recorded in American literature, suggests one reason why the hoped-for cultural synthesis in that area has not yet been realized— an incompatibility of value systems. Not only was there a considerable difference in outlook between the great Mexican landowners and the

Americans who poured in to occupy the Southwest after the Mexican-American War of 1846–1847, but there was a substantial difference in attitudes toward the land between these Americans and the poor and humble Mexican "peasants" who had worked their lands for centuries before the arrival of the Americans. In his cultural history of the New Mexico-South Texas region entitled *Rio Grande*, Fergusson analyzes this difference:

> These owners of tiny farms were sometimes called paisanos—men of the country, men of the soil. And true peasants they are, perhaps the only ones that ever existed within our borders. For the peasant is a lover of the earth who asks nothing better than to live his whole life on one patch of soil, scratching it for a living, laying his bones in it at last. And there has never been much of this resigned sedentary spirit in the American farmer of the Anglo-Saxon breed. He was originally a wanderer and always an exploiter. He settles down only when there is no place else to go. He does not cherish the earth, he loves to conquer it. Always he tends to exhaust the soil and move on, whether in a few years or a few generations, as did the tobacco planters in Virginia, the cotton planters farther south. His interest is always in a "money crop." He believes in progress and longs for change.[7]

Other American writers have remarked about differences in feelings about the land between Mexican and Anglo-American. In *Our America* the novelist Waldo Frank says of the Mexican that, not having the restless and exploitative ambition of the Anglo-American, he was not an "ideal pioneer." Instead "he became attached to his soil and loved it and drew pleasure and drew beauty from it." The Mexican's adobe house, according to Frank, "gives us his inner life. Here a man has settled down and sought happiness with his surroundings: sought life by cultivation rather than exploitation."

Fergusson has made the point that for the Mexican the land is loved for itself, not as a means of profit or "progress." The Southwestern writer Frank Waters vivifies this aspect of Mexican psychology in his novel *People of the Valley.* An old Mexican matriarch, Maria del Valle, has become increasingly suspicious and disgruntled at plans to build a dam which would flood the immediate vicinity of the valley but which would, it has been pointed out to her, provide a steady water supply for the surrounding area. The valley has for centuries been subject to periodic droughts, disastrous to the people. In order for this dam to be built, however, the people would have to sell their lands to the American government, at a good price, and move elsewhere. This is the "catch," and it catches at the throat of the people, who are torn between the desire for the immediate cash, as well as their sense of the benefits the dam would bring, and the ancient sense of their own *tierra*. Maria explains to a local judge her feeling about the situation:

> I do not oppose the dam, new customs, a new vision of life; I oppose nothing. But I uphold the old ways for they are good too. I awaken in men their love for their land for they are a people of the land. It is their faith. And so I place their faith above all the lesser benefits they might derive from that which would oppose it.[8]

When the government forces the issue, Maria will not move and dies upon her *tierra* as the dam is being constructed.

Incompatibility between Mexican and Anglo-American culture extends beyond questions of the land. It crops up in a number of important and emotionally fraught areas of life, and the expression of these differences can be traced to a number of fundamental divergences in temperament and philosophical outlook. American anthropologists such as William Madsen have made some general observations about such divergences. Among them have been the assertion that among Mexican Americans suffering is made acceptable because of a strain of fatalism in their culture, that there is among them an element of resignation resulting in a lack of drive. Other observations include the notions that the Anglo controls while the Mexican accepts, that the Anglo tries to overcome misfortune while the Latin views it as fate, that the Anglo is rational while the Mexican is basically emotional. Chicano activists, on their part, have countered these generalities by claiming that they amount to stereotyping on the part of Anglo-American academics.

Some American writers have taken a positive view of differences in matters of social and cultural expression. To Mary Austin, the Mexican mode of life was clearly superior because it more deeply satisfied profound human needs. She remarked that anyone who had seen a religious procession on the streets of Santa Fe would have

> the key to much in our English-speaking life that is mortifying and confusing. For what do our Kiwanis and Ku-Kluxers seek, with their make-up school-boy titles and their pillow cases, but to recapture the lost art of expressing dramatically the fundamental life relations which, here in our Southwest, flow naturally into forms born of the great age of Dante and Lope de Vega?"[9]

The American philosopher F. S. C. Northrop describes the essence of the culture conflict between Mexican and Anglo-American and indicates the need for synthesis.

What impresses as novel in Mexican culture is its highly developed appreciation of the aesthetic and its religion of the emotions; and what the Mexicans fear in the merging of their culture with that of the United States is that the latter excessively pragmatic, economically centered culture will, in its zeal for its own values, overwhelm and destroy the cultural assets of the Indian-and-Latin world. But this task of relating aesthetic and emotionally immediate religious values to scientific, doctrinal, and pragmatic values is precisely what constitutes the fundamental problem.[10]

The ceremonial aspect of social life among Mexicans and Mexican-Americans is reflected in the individual deportment of people who are products of Mexican culture. The Mexican sets a high value upon *dignidad* as a part of his personal style. He must act himself and be treated by others in accordance with a strong sense of personal honor and dignity. His mode of conduct, therefore, has not only an element of gravity but also a certain grace, deriving from a feeling for the ceremonious. To the Mexican or Mexican-American, typical American boisterousness, however good-humored or essentially innocent, is distasteful. Latin humor does not typically express itself in horseplay.

Latin attitudes toward fate, as well as the emotional, intuitive, and ceremonial approach to life, have another philosophical consequence, or perhaps source. The Brazilian novelist Erico Verissimo has said that the differences between North Americans and Latin Americans can be summed up by the infinitives "to do" and "to be," and part of the aspect of being is the acceptance of assigned roles.

One expression of the Latin's sense of working out such a role is a dedication to the concept of family life. A powerful social unit among Mexican-Americans, the family consists not only of the immediate family but also of what anthropologists call the extended family, which includes all relatives on both sides. Perhaps this sense of family solidarity against the world has derived from the history of Latin American politics, which in sometimes riding roughshod over individuals may well have given them a sense of personal insecurity and driven them back for protection upon the only trustworthy group, the family. In terms of their experience in the United States, Mexican-Americans may have felt this sense of insecurity heightened by an awareness of prejudice against them.

Since the primary loyalty is conceived of as belonging to the family, removing oneself from the family, physically or socially or occupationally, can be thought of as an act of disloyalty. Therefore, the sense of fealty to the family can act as an inhibiting factor to the young Mexican-

American who is in search of employment. The search should not go far afield. Since the rags-to-riches theme is central to the North American mythos and takes primacy over any sense of confinement to a locality, we have here another case of difference in value systems.

Among the values prized by Mexican and Mexican-American males is the celebrated sense of machismo. It is possible that North Americans may have an exaggerated sense of the power of this concept among Latin men, but it is undeniably a factor. This concept of machismo contains a constellation of ideas, but certainly among them is the prizing of sexual virility, a potency whose practice is not necessarily to be confined to the home.

American literature has taken note of the intensity of Mexican sexual life. The early chronicles of the Southwest, such as Josiah Gregg's *Commerce of the Prairies,* Lewis Garrard's *Wah-To-Yah and the Taos Trail,* and James Josiah Webb's *Adventures in the Santa Fe Trade,* have condemned this activity as evidence of promiscuity and depravity among the Mexicans. Modern American writers, sometimes engaged in a campaign against American "puritanism," have praised the Mexican for his earthiness, vitality, and freedom from enervating inhibitions. Bernard DeVoto, in *1846: The Year of Decision,* twits an early Southwestern chronicler, Susan Magoffin, for her prudishness before the realities of Mexican life. "Susan could not approve," he wrote, "the abandon of those dances in which the women were so fervently embraced. She was not reconciled to the native costumes which, though prettily colored, were not reticent about a woman's limbs and exposed so much of the bosom that Susan turned her eyes from what she considered open incitation of the baser instincts."[11] John Steinbeck's *Tortilla Flat* is but one of a number of modern American novels which praise the Mexican for the richness of his sexual life.

Though modern American novelists and poets have tended to extol the Mexican for his personalism, his emotional intensity, his sense of tradition, and his avoidance of many of the tinsel artificialities of modern American life, some American social scientists have noted aspects of Mexican culture or personality which tend to work against the Mexican-Americans in the general American society in which they must make their way. For example, business relations among Mexicans are sometimes tinged with subjective attitudes and personal feeling. The psychologist Arnold Meadow, in reporting upon the results of his research, has compared ways of handling situations in banking among Mexicans, Mexican-Americans, and Anglo-Americans. Among the Mexicans such values as personal friendship weigh heavily and are often more important than questions of efficiency or objective treatment of customers. Among Mexican-Americans in banking an acute culture conflict is sometimes experienced, especially at first, before a reluctant adjustment is made in the direction of Anglo-American standards of objective, dispassionate, and efficient treatment of people and affairs. Dr. Meadow comments that perhaps Mexican-Americans, in making their adjustment to Anglo ways, are losing important human values. However, one might add that not only efficiency but probably justice is gained in the exchange.

Much of the foregoing had devoted itself to a review of value conflicts between Mexican-Americans and Anglo-Americans. What, then, of the synthesis envisioned by Walt Whitman, by Mary Austin, and by Charles F. Lummis? In certain undeniable ways, Mexico has already left its impress upon the American Southwest. In rural areas, especially, Mexican influence is strong even though often unacknowledged. It is visible in many facets of daily life, in the mud adobe bricks used for building, in fences made of mesquite branches, in food, in place-names, and in the words used for common articles of daily usage. It is especially strong in anything to do with the raising and marketing of cattle, that basic and traditional industry of the Southwest. The Mexican vaquero or cowboy was a type developed in over three hundred years of conditioning in a highly specialized environment. He passed on his techniques, vocabulary, and lore to the Anglo-American cattlemen of the Southwest. In *The King Ranch,* Tom Lea writes:

> The Mexican vaqueros became the prototypes who furnished the ready-made tools, the range techniques, even the lingo, from which sprang the cowboy of song and story. The Mexican haciendas provided the primal outlines for the pattern which produced the later cattle kingdom of the American West.[12]

Edward Larocque Tinker, in his book *The Horseman of the Americas and the Literature They Inspired,* also acknowledges the valuable apprenticeship which the American cowboy received at the hands of the Mexican vaquero. He goes into considerable detail about vocabulary, listing a number of word borrowings.

And the mining industry in the Southwest received not only techniques but also vocabulary from the Mexicans, including mining's most famous word, *bonanza.* In *The Big Bonanza,* Dan De Quille devoted three pages to a glossary of Mexican mining terms in general use in the Washoe country. In his linguistic and, by extension, sociological study, *A Diction-*

*ary of Spanish Terms in English with Special Reference to the American South-west,* Harold W. Bentley records the impressive amount of language borrowing that has occurred.

Many communities in the Southwest, in their architecture and community layouts, bear the stamp of Mexican influence. In that early classic of American writing on Mexico, *Viva Mexico!,* Charles M. Flandrau writes of the Mexican plaza in a way that could be applied to many a South-western town, such as Santa Fe and San Antonio:

> The plaza is in constant use from morning until late at night. . . . By eleven o'clock at night the whole town will, at various hours, have passed through it, strolled in it, played, sat, rested, talked, or thought in it. . . . The plaza is a sort of social clearinghouse—a resource—a solution. I know of nothing quite like it, and nothing as fertile in the possibilities of innocent diversion.[13]

Certainly, borrowings from Mexican culture there have been aplenty. But, as Flandrau said elsewhere in his book, all too often the Americans will "accept the best of everything in Mexico" and yet "stupidly deny its attraction for them, repudiate their sympathy with it." If the Mexican is himself rejected or "invisible" in the Southwest despite the many physical and linguistic reminders of his presence, despite the fact that it is he who has given real savor to the land, are there still possibilities of any significant cultural fusion? The value conflicts are indeed there. Any real rapprochement will require a moving toward each other from both sides. Here again, the novelists have spoken.

In *People of the Valley,* Frank Waters presents a character who exhibits a subtle fusion of two cultures. He is Don Eliseo, a Mexican-American judge. He understands and respects much of the ideal of impersonal justice stemming from the English common law, and he also understands deeply the subjectivism and personalism of his own people. Standing astride two traditions, he is a successful mediator between the two cultures because he has formed within himself a working synthesis. Old Maria del Valle, in rebuking a granddaughter for having mocked the "gringos," says:

> Yes, they are ignorant of some things as we Spanish-Americans are ignorant of others. So do not condemn them unjustly. When we both see all, then will there be no difference between us. . . . The good judge; was he not a ragged little chamaco? Is he not respected now by the Anglos perhaps more than by us? Simply because his eyes, through learning, have seen both ways.[14]

Harvey Fergusson treats the subject of cultural synthesis in *The Conquest of Don Pedro,* a delightful and significant novel of New Mexico in transition. A Jewish shopkeeper, Leo Mendes, representing an unsung type of Western pioneer, takes an interest in a bright Mexican girl, Magdalena, while she is still a child. Leo, not without some qualms, begins giving the girl reading matter of a scientific and natural history type, of which he knows her parents will not approve. In thinking of the probable future of quick-minded Magdalena, Leo feels a kind of resignation.

> By the time she was sixteen . . . she might be married, often to a husband chosen by her parents and always to one approved by them. Mexican women in general accepted this destiny with grace and resignation, as the will of God, but Leo felt that it was probably going to be difficult for Magdalena, with her rebellious temper, her love of action and her versatile curiosity. For curiosity in particular there seemed to be no place in a life of faith and status. It was essentially an unquestioning life.[15]

However, when Magdalena marries, it is to Leo himself, her mentor. Yet in a matter of a few years Magdalena becomes totally absorbed in a young and impressive-looking Texan named Robert Coppinger. He is from people who are "much like her own in everything but race—cattle people who own the earth and have the habit of command." With characteristic detachment, Leo recognizes that his relationship with Magdalena has always been essentially paternal. He makes way for the younger man. Magdalena represents the result of the impact of two cultures. Leo Mendes, the wandering Jew, was for her a kind of catalytic agent between these two societies. Without consciously meaning to exploit him, she sought him instinctively as the way to freedom, and under his guidance she achieved in her personality a synthesis which might well represent the author's vision of an eventual cultural fusion in the Southwest.

The change in Magdalena was in the form of adjustment to Anglo-American life. In *Rio Grande,* Fergusson considers the other side, the strength of Mexican influence. He describes the Mexican as "unmistakably . . . an emergent type" who is "beginning to grasp the tools of industrial civilization" and to "find himself in the arts." The Mexican "track-workers and fruit pickers" in the Southwest are "pioneers," and so are "the Mexican painters and cartoonists who invade the literary teas in Manhattan. Indo-Spanish America is coming toward us, bringing both its gifts and its needs."[16] It seems likely that the growing recognition of the power of Mexican culture and the uniqueness of its art will result in an increase of Mexican cultural influence in the American Southwest.

Meanwhile, a growing Mexican middle class, no longer inept in the ways of commerce and increasingly making its influence felt in political life, seems firmly decided to take its destiny into its own hands.

# 6

## Mexican Painters and American Writers

The Mexican Revolution, beginning in 1910, jarred the United States out of its usual complacent disregard for its neighbor to the south, a disregard which was later to settle back in place until recent flurries of concern over drug shipments across the border. That the Revolution caused a stir in the art world in the United States, there can be no doubt. "The wind that swept Mexico" sent its shock waves northward. The impact that they made included the powerful influence of the cultural renaissance in Mexico which followed the actual fighting but which was very much a product of the Revolution. The bold Mexican painting of the period, because it obviated the language barrier, was the first cultural medium to make its announcements heard up north.

In 1922, a group of prominent Mexican artists, together with the American writer Katherine Anne Porter, assembled a collection of over eighty thousand pieces of Mexican Indian art, dating from pre-Columbian times to the twentieth century. The plan was to mount a large exhibit to be shown throughout the United States. The original scheme was thwarted by politics, as the collection was stopped at the border by American customs officials reacting to the fact that the government of President Alvaro Obregón was not recognized by the United States. That the exhibit was held at all was due to a Los Angeles dealer who bought the entire collection himself, paid the customs duties, and brought it to Los Angeles. The show opened on November 10 and was an instant success. As to the long-range influence of the show, Porter was later to claim that "all the tremendous interest in Mexican art stemmed from that [show]." As a guide to the exhibit, Katherine Anne Porter published an impressive monograph, *Outline of Popular Mexican Arts and Crafts.*

Two aspects of this episode are of particular interest. The first is that the emphasis was upon Indian art. In its very principle of selection, the exhibit carried one of the most important messages of the Mexican Revolution. Mexico was at last to come to terms with its deeply rooted Indian heritage. The second is that the organizing spirit behind the exhibit was an American literary figure soon to emerge, largely through the inspiration of her Mexican experience, as an important figure in modern American literature. The art of the Mexican Revolution, therefore, is shown to have had a direct impact upon modern American literature. In fact, the powerful murals of Diego Rivera were so to affect the sensibility of Katherine Anne Porter that they were to determine the very way that she saw Mexico. In turn, the Mexican scene was to provide the inspiration for those early stories which established Porter as a prime exponent of the modern American short story.

Katherine Anne Porter is quite explicit about the effects that Rivera's paintings had upon her: "For myself, and I believe I speak for great numbers, Mexico does not appear to me as it did before I saw Rivera's paintings of it. The mountains, the Indians, the horses, the flowers and children, have all subtly changed in outlines and colors. They are Rivera's Indians and flowers and all now. . . ." Porter's biographer, Joan Givner, explains that Porter transferred the concepts that she had developed about Mexican art into the aesthetic theories that governed her writing: "Ever afterward she incorporated her ideas on Mexican art into her own aesthetic theory, expressing frequently, in her discussions of her own work, the opinion that the artist must draw his strength from his roots and from his familiar world."

In addition to Porter, there were three other American women who, in this early period of the discovery of Mexican art, were to make the American public aware of what was probably the most important movement in world painting at that time. Anita Brenner in 1929 published a book which has since become famous. *Idols Behind Altars* traces the pervasive influence of indigenous art forms throughout the entire history of Mexican art, including the work of the great painters of the Mexican Revolution, Rivera, Orozco, Siqueiros, and—though less immediately influenced by the Revolution—Tamayo. Alma Reed, whose personal life was so closely involved with those important figures of Mexico, wrote two biographies of José Clemente Orozco. Mary Austin, whose books on the American Southwest—written in the early 1900s—are now enjoying a revival of interest, received a sort of second wind in her writing as a result of the influence of Diego Rivera. According to her biographer, Augusta Fink:

> She was especially impressed by Rivera, both the man and his work. His murals moved her to tears. In them she saw patterns of color and emotion, of compassion and community, that she had tried to express in *American Rhythm*. So beneficial was the Mexican interlude that she returned feeling better able to work than she had in almost a decade.

The American novelist John Dos Passos went to Mexico in the mid 1920s and again in 1932. He was immensely captivated by the Mexican muralists and saw the significance of their work to the literary plans that were already forming in his mind. His article "Paint the Revolution!," published in *New Masses* of March 1927, surveyed the work of Rivera, Orozco, and Montenegro. He also explained in a memoir the direct way in which the Mexican muralists influenced the development of his famous trilogy: "I was trying to organize some of these stories I picked up in Mexico into the intertwined narratives that later became *The 42nd Parallel*. *Three Soldiers* and *Manhattan Transfer* had been single panels; now, somewhat as the Mexican painters felt compelled to paint their walls, I felt compelled to start on a narrative panorama to which I saw no end." In *The 42nd Parallel*, one of the characters, Mac, a former Wobbly, goes down into revolutionary Mexico, makes contact with labor groups there, and finally marries and settles down in the country.

The Southwestern novelist Harvey Fergusson saw the impact of the Mexican painters upon the United States within the wider context of the "reverse frontier" by which Mexico, having been defeated by the United States in 1848, is reasserting its influence in areas of the United States which had once belonged to it, as well as in regions well beyond the Southwest. He saw both the humble Mexican laborers and the important Mexican painters as exerting their separate forms of influence. His remarks, though written during the period of the Mexican Revolution, still bear upon the effects of the upward thrusting influence from south of the border.

# 7

## American Writers in Mexico, 1875-1925

Since the fourth decade of the nineteenth century, Mexico has been, for the United States, a presence that cannot be ignored. By the close of the fifth decade, the United States had absorbed, through conquest, approximately half of Mexico's original territory. In doing so, it assured that it would have within its own vitals representatives of a culture that it was to find very difficult to comprehend. Yet by the very pressure of its presence, Mexico has challenged the writers of the United States to react to it in one way or another.

The first contacts that engendered literary responses were in the borderland regions. It was to take some time before American writers were to make their way into the heart of Mexico, and by the time they did so, a tradition for them of American writing about Mexico had already been established, either to confirm or to confront. The early borderland writers were not, on the whole, writers in the professional sense. They were frontiersmen, soldiers, government agents, traders, the wives of any of these, or just plain travelers. Their very amateur standing as writers, however, gave them a particular usefulness for our own times. They were not, as are so many literary people, a type apart. It now seems clear that, in their reactions to an alien culture, they reflected quite tellingly the attitudes and biases of their times. In doing so, they rendered a more revealing portrait, it would seem, of the America of their time than they did of Mexico.

Nineteenth-century America, in its puritanism, its optimism based on a belief in progress through science, its ethnocentricity and racial pride, and its frontier egalitarianism, was affronted by a Mexico which seemed sinful and self-indulgent, backward, mongrelized, and hierarchical. The stereotypes of the Mexican produced by the borderland chronicles written during the period of the Texas Revolution and of the Mexican-American War and its aftermath were to sink deeply into the national consciousness of the United States, where they reside today among a great many of its inhabitants.

Events within the United States and Mexico, which occurred simultaneously, had the effect of suspending communication for the better part of a decade as the two nations turned inward in their preoccupation with their own problems. In the United States, the sectional tensions of the late 1850s and early 1860s over the issues of slavery and economic rivalries led to the unparalleled carnage of the Civil War. In Mexico, a bloody civil war between the Liberals and the Conservatives resulted in the emergence of Benito Juárez as the great reform leader in the 1850s. But the Conservatives engendered the intervention of Emperor Napoleon III of France, whose troops in the 1860s placed Maximilian upon the throne of Mexico as emperor. The resurgent Juaristas, with some help from President Lincoln's government, eventually forced the French out. In 1867, by order of President Juárez, Maximilian was executed in Querétaro. Two transformed nations were ready to resume relationships.

The post-Civil War era in the United States was to prove to be a watershed period. A nation which had been predominantly rural, Anglo-Saxon, and Protestant became rapidly transformed into an urbanized, industrialized, multinational and multicultural country. The effect of these changes upon the "soul" of the nation was immense. As uprooted rural populations poured into the factories of the big cities, immigrant masses, even more uprooted, pursued, in grime and toil, the American dream. The word *alienation* came into the American vocabulary.

In a considerably more chastened mood, American writers were prepared to look toward a neighboring culture with attitudes quite different from the cocksure condescension and racism of the earlier borderland writers. In fact, a neighbor to the south which had managed to preserve a culture in depth was to exert a positive attraction.

In 1872 the American poet and journalist William Cullen Bryant went to Mexico as part of a Latin American journey. It is not surprising that his reactions to the Mexican scene were in definite contrast with those of the borderland chroniclers. In addition to being a cultivated man of letters,

he was by origin a New Englander. His native Massachusetts was note-
worthy for being against the grain in the period of Manifest Destiny and
the Mexican-American War. For New England intellectuals and writers,
the war was an imperialist venture, and they looked upon President
James Polk, a Southerner, with extreme suspicion. Such writers as Emerson, Thoreau, Channing, and Lowell viewed the war as a covert effort to
extend the slave territories. Though Bryant's puritan sensibilities led him
to condemn such things as the lottery, the bullfight, and clerical corruption in Mexico, he was strongly struck by the figure of Benito Juárez, in
his dignity, integrity, and strong idealism. Also, in marked contrast with
the borderland writers, Bryant approved the rise of the Indian and mestizo in Mexican society. While attending a meeting of the Geographical
and Statistical Society in Mexico City, a society devoted to cultivation of
the arts and sciences, Bryant took note of the vice president of Mexico,
Ramírez, and the distinguished Mexican historian, Altamirano, both
Indians. These examples of men of indigenous stock who had risen to
positions of eminence in Mexico occasioned him to write in the essay "A
Visit to Mexico" that "many of these descendents of the people subdued
by Cortes are men of cultivated minds and engaging manners. The
greater part of the works of art in the galleries of which I have spoken
[Mexican Academy of Arts] are from their hands."

The literary achievements of Mexico did not go unnoticed by Bryant.
He translated nine of the "Fábulas" by the poet José Rosas Moreno,
thus being the first major American poet to recognize the achievements
of Mexican poetry. Bryant also carried on a correspondence with the
poet Guillermo Prieto, who, incidentally, was Juárez's secretary of the
treasury.

President Benito Juárez died in office and, after a brief interregnum, a
new leader rose to power who was to rule Mexico dictatorially for thirty
years. This man was General Porfirio Díaz, and his long reign has come to
be known as the Porfiriato. Ironically, the dictator was directly a product
of the man who most urgently sought the rule of law for Mexico, Benito
Juárez. Díaz was the most effective of Juárez's generals, but clearly he did
not share, at least after he rose to power, his mentor's ideals. But the
Porfiriato became very attractive to many Americans. In his desire to
modernize Mexico, Díaz granted many concessions to American busi-
nessmen and developers. For writers one of the attractions was the new
safety that the Porfiriato had brought to travelers in Mexico. Díaz's elite
paramilitary police force, the famous *rurales*, brought law and order to

the remotest corners of the country. American writers now felt that they could penetrate with impunity into the interior regions of Mexico.

Some came principally in search of local color, as was the case with Charles Dudley Warner, whose principal claim to literary fame was his coauthorship with Mark Twain of the novel *The Gilded Age.* Warner records his adventures in a group of sketches called *On Horseback,* published in 1888. Many of the colorful aspects of the country delighted him, but in some respects he seems to be a throwback to the early chroniclers, particularly in his inveighing against miscegenation among the population. A more penetrating writer on Mexico was the famous Western painter Frederick Remington. As might be expected, the pictorial splendor of the country caught his eye. In his account of travels through northern Mexico, *Pony Tracks* (1895), Remington reveals that much of the attraction of the great open country of Sonora was prompted by his full-scale reaction against the growing mechanization of life in the United States. For Remington, the hard-riding vaqueros of northern Mexico were splendid examples of adaptation to terrain and of freedom and virility.

The first important American fiction writer to enter Mexico and to draw upon Mexican materials was Stephen Crane. In the mid 1890s he was sent to the Southwest and to Mexico by a newspaper syndicate. The very fact of this sponsorship would argue an awakened public interest in Mexico. Crane was one of the first American writers to sound a note which was to be added to and enlarged upon by a number of modern American writers. As a countertheme to a pride in newness, the Whitmanesque proclaiming of the American Adam, there has been in American letters a deep undercurrent of yearning, a need for a "usable past." The effort to conjure up such a past has occupied American writers from the later nineteenth century until the present. It is here that American writers have looked upon Mexico with something of envy. The Mexican past stretches back to the great Indian civilizations of the Mayas and Aztecs, and the modern Mexican, unlike the provincially race-proud Anglo-Saxon, carries, in the genes and in the historic memory, the Indian past. Furthermore, a hundred years before the Pilgrims arrived at Plymouth Rock, the Spanish Empire had established itself in Mexico. Crane manages to convey a sense of all this in the following description of a great highway:

The Paseo de la Reforma is the famous drive of the City of Mexico, leading to the castle of Chapultepec, which last ought to be well known in the

United States. It is a broad, fine avenue of macadam, with a much greater quality of dignity than anything of the kind we possess in our land. It seems of the Old World, where to the beauty of the thing itself is added the solemnity of tradition and history, cavalcades of steel thundered there before the coming of carriages.

Crane wrote a series of articles about his Mexican experiences which appeared in the *Philadelphia Press,* beginning in 1895. He also wrote six short stories with Mexican locales. These pieces combined shrewd and sensitively rendered observation with a good deal of stereotyping. One of the characters in the Mexico City stories, the New York Kid—no doubt a projection of Crane himself—seems always to be triumphing over cruel and cowardly Mexican connivers. One of the best of these stories, "Horses One-Dash," deals with an American, Richardson, with his Mexican guide attempting to outrun a group of pursuing bandits. The psychological study of flight and fear is masterful—and reminiscent of *The Red Badge of Courage.* Even this tale is somewhat marred by the sort of stereotyping mentioned above. Yet Crane's American heroes in Mexico, unlike the crude Anglo-Saxon swaggerers of the dime novels and Texas romances so popular in an earlier day, are treated with a light irony that suggests parody.

Probably the best book about Mexico written by an American during the Porfiriato is now almost forgotten. *Viva Mexico!,* by Charles M. Flandrau, is the author's account of life on a coffee plantation in the state of Vera Cruz together with his observations about the Mexican scene in general. The very fact of American ownership of a coffee plantation in southern Mexico was an indication of the Porfiriato's generosity toward foreigners, a generosity often practiced at the expense of native Mexicans. But *Viva Mexico!* is essentially apolitical. It is instead a sophisticated, sympathetic, and often humorous study of manners. Flandrau says in his book that the best work about Mexico ever written by a foreigner was Fanny Calderón de la Barca's *Life in Mexico,* written by the Scottish wife of Spain's first ambassador to the new republic of Mexico. The fact is that Flandrau's book itself ranks with the classic work that he mentions with such admiration. Fanny Calderón wrote her account during the years 1840–1841, while Flandrau's book was published in 1910. Yet, as Flandrau points out, the Mexican society that he was observing was essentially that which Fanny Calderón had known. Despite Juárez's reform laws and the extensive modernization brought about by Porfirio Díaz, the old Creole (*criollo*) feudalistic society remained pretty much intact.

What Flandrau did not know, and what gives his book its special poignancy, was that he was writing on the very eve of the great "wind that swept Mexico," the revolution that was to shatter the Porfiriato and change the face of Mexican society. And yet for all of this, the old French adage still applies: "The more things change, the more they remain the same." There is much in Flandrau's book that is still recognizable in present-day Mexico. Shortly after Flandrau's arrival in Vera Cruz, a lady said to him, "No hay reglas fijas, señor" (There are no fixed rules, sir). The author was to adopt this statement as his motto for Mexico. By way of explanation Flandrau goes on to write:

> A well-regulated, systematic, and precise person always detests Mexico and can rarely bring himself to say a kind word about anything in it, including the scenery. But if one is not inclined to exaggerate the importance of exactitude and is perpetually interested in the casual, the florid, and the problematic, Mexico is one, long, carelessly written but absorbing romance.[1]

In contrast with the endless complaints by the border chroniclers to the effect that Mexico had depreciated its racial stock by allowing Europeans to mix with the Indians, Flandrau says: "In its way, the mixture of Spaniard with tropical Indian—which was the original recipe for making the contemporary Mexican—is physically a pleasing one. It isn't our way, but one doesn't after a while find it less attractive for that."

Being a foreigner himself, Flandrau was particularly alert to the situation of foreigners in Mexico. He estimated—and this was due to Díaz's policy of bringing in foreign capital and technology—that there were thirty thousand Americans resident in Mexico during his stay. Many of them were managers of mines, plantations, and railroads. He winced at the many American tourists he encountered and wrote of them very much in the vein of Mark Twain's *Innocents Abroad*.

Flandrau comments on the Americans' insistence on denigrating things Mexican even when secretly enjoying them:

> I have often been amused and depressed by the manner in which foreigners [and he is particularly referring to Americans here] who accept the best of everything in Mexico—who grow strong, and revel in one of its several climates, who make a good living there, who enjoy its beauty and adopt many of its customs—stupidly deny its attraction for them, repudiate their sympathy with it.[2]

As for himself, Flandrau, in marked contrast with a number of the earlier American writers on Mexico, attuned himself to the nuances of that country and led the way to a new American perception of Mexico. A good example of his recognition of the currents that make up Mexican life is his commentary about the role of the plaza in Mexican society:

> The plaza is in constant use from morning until late at night. Ladies stop there on their way home from church, "dar una vuelta" (to take a turn), as they call it, and to see and be seen; gentlemen frequently interrupt the labors of the day by going there to meditate over a cigar; schoolboys find in it a shady, secluded bench and use it as a study; nurse maids use it as a nursery; children use its broad, outside walks as a playground; tired workmen use it as a place of rest. By eleven o'clock at night the whole town will, at various hours, have passed through it, strolled in it, played, sat, rested, talked, or thought in it, . . . The plaza is a kind of social clearing house—a resource—a solution. I know nothing quite like it, and nothing as fertile in the possibilities of innocent diversion.[3]

In 1910, President Porfirio Díaz decreed a lavish display and endless rounds of parties to celebrate his thirtieth year in power. The many foreign officials invited to Mexico City for the occasion were immensely impressed. From their point of view, Díaz was unquestionably the greatest president Mexico had ever had. Díaz then proceeded once again to rig the electoral machinery in Mexico to ensure his reelection. But things unaccountably began to go awry. A slightly built man from the northern state of Coahuila, a man with a squeaky voice and vegetarian conviction—the type of man whom the virile Porfirio Díaz could never bring himself to take seriously—began to talk publicly about an opposition party and about the principle of no reelection, a position that Díaz himself had once espoused. Wherever he went, Francisco I. Madero began to draw immense crowds. Before long, he had formed a political party and found himself with young, fierce, self-commissioned officers at his service. Among them was Doroteo Arango, better known as Pancho Villa. The systematically weakened federal army (Don Porfirio had weeded out all potential rivals) rode north only to be cracked open by the hard-riding vaqueros fighting for Francisco Madero. Simultaneously in the south, the Indians, whose fields had been taken over by rich landowners during the Porfiriato, rose under the indomitable Emiliano Zapata. Porfirio Díaz dashed to a boat which would take him to exile in France. The great revolution was on.

The Porfiriato had made Mexico into a modern nation, but it had done so at the cost of aggrandizing a relatively small group of native and foreign industrialists at the expense of the masses of the people. In addition, the communal Indian villages, free since colonial times, were now taken over—with the acquiescence of the regime—by the great landed estates. Once-free men and women were now subjected to the lash. Neither Díaz nor his *científicos* seemed to have concerned themselves with the nether side of the gilded Porfiriato.

The revolution which followed was different from any Latin American revolution which had yet occurred. It was not the overturning of one set of betasseled generals by another. It was a profound shaking up of the entire society. When rumbles of it crossed the border into the United States, some people were frightened, whereas other were exhilarated. Among the latter were American writers with radical tendencies.

Jack London crossed into Mexico, excited by the ozone of social cataclysm. He wrote letters and dispatches expressing his revolutionary ardor. On August 19, 1911, his story "The Mexican" appeared in the *Saturday Evening Post* (later reprinted in *The Night Born*, 1913). The story deals with a young Mexican, Felipe Rivera, who boxed in Los Angeles, having to deal with ring officials who were prejudiced against his race. His fight earnings were donated to a junta in Los Angeles which was supporting the Mexican Revolution. John Reed was also deeply stirred, and for a while he followed the armies of Villa, at considerable peril to himself, sending home reports. He wrote two Mexican stories, "Mac-American" and "Endymion," published in 1914 and 1916 in *Masses*. (They were reprinted in *Daughters of the Revolution* in 1927). "Endymion" dealt with a borderlands doctor who would charge no more than a quarter for any medical service and who was sympathetic to the Mexican revolutionaries. "Mac-American" reported on the conversation of three Americans in a bar in Chihuahua. They decry the Mexicans as people without heart while revealing their sympathies to lynching in the American South. These stories, though revealing a genuineness of feeling, are to a considerable extent propagandistic. Reed's collected articles and sketches on the Mexican Revolution finally appeared in a volume entitled *Insurgent Mexico* (1969). The journalist Lincoln Steffens, described by Drewey Wayne Gunn as a "less impassioned but more prestigious defender of the Mexican Revolution than Reed," made three trips to revolutionary Mexico, interviewed prominent leaders, and sent home a good deal of copy. His several short stories with Mexican locales are now largely historical curiosities. A final legend of the period, in terms of American literature, was to be bestowed by Ambrose Bierce. After having confided to his daughter his sympathy with the Mexican Revolution, he crossed into Mexico in 1913, never to be seen again.

The American writers who were actually at the scene of the fighting itself were to play their most important role in paving the way for

American writers of greater talents. Once the news about insurgent Mexico had been brought to America, people in the arts became alerted to a consequence of this insurgency: the Mexican renaissance in literature and painting, which began to flower in the 1920s. Clearly the most important and influential of the American writers who were to draw upon this renaissance was Katherine Anne Porter.

Though in due time Katherine Anne Porter was to see plenty of Paris, she once said significantly about her formative years as a writer that "Mexico City was my Paris." Her upbringing in Texas, and particularly the periods of time she spent in San Antonio, established her first contacts with Mexican culture, but her first significant contact with the Mexican art world occurred in Greenwich Village in New York City, where a number of Mexican artists had gathered toward the close of the first decade of the twentieth century. Most important of these, for Porter, was Adolpho Best-Maugard, who instructed her in the traditions of Mexican art and culture. He procured for her the commission to write the story for a Mexican ballet, for which he was to do the scenery. The chief dancer was to be none other than Pavlova. As a result of this and related activities, Porter began to get a reputation for knowledgeability about things Mexican. On the basis of this, she was offered in 1920 a job with *Magazine of Mexico,* a promotional magazine backed by American bankers. The lure of this assignment was that she had to go to Mexico itself for materials. Thus began a series of visits and periods of living in Mexico which lasted until 1931. Her biographer, Joan Givner, describes Katherine Anne Porter's first trip through the Mexican countryside toward Mexico City:

> When she got off the train one evening in Chihuahua and looked at the roof, she saw bayonetted rifles silhouetted against the sky, and smoke rising from the hot braziers of what resembled a militarized kitchen. Traveling on through war-ravaged land, she saw the charred ruins of the old hacienda mansions and, in the large towns, whole buildings which had been leveled by cannon fire or burned by the peons. The walls of most of the buildings were densely pocked with bullets and plastered with slogans.[4]

By the time she reached Mexico City, the spectacle of the Mexican Revolution had been deeply etched into her being.

It was this first experience in Mexico that turned the key for Porter as a literary artist. She herself partook of the released creative energies which the revolution had tapped. Of her publication of the story "María Concepción" in *Century Illustrated Magazine* in 1922, Joan Givner says: "She was indeed launched." Givern also gives an account of Porter working all night to finish her most famous Mexican story:

> She may not have been fully aware of the achievement but she was exhilarated by her night's work and did not wait for morning to send it off. At one thirty in the morning she was standing on a snowy, windy corner putting it into the mailbox to Lincoln Kirstein, the editor of *Hound and Horn*. The story was "Flowering Judas" and it made her literary reputation.[5]

Though Katherine Anne Porter was fully aware that the Revolution had released the energies for the Mexican renaissance in the arts, she did not share the uncritical admiration for the Revolution that characterized Reed and Steffens. Undoubtedly this was true to some measure because she saw not the fighting itself but the aftermath. Of the Mexican stories, "That Tree," "Flowering Judas," and "Hacienda" deal with the theme of the Revolution's having been betrayed by its own leaders. She had seen the feet of clay on some of its most famous proponents, such as Diego Rivera, and had become quite familiar with the phenomenon of former revolutionary generals gorged with the spoils that were to have been divided among the country's poor. In "Hacienda," Don Genaro, the owner of the hacienda that gave title to the story (haciendas supposedly having been abolished by the Revolution), is exasperated with a local judge for arresting his peons and asking payments to have them released. Don Genaro decides to turn to a powerful ex-revolutionary in Mexico City:

> Everybody agreed with him that Velarde was the man to see. He was the most powerful and successful revolutionist in Mexico. He owned two pulque haciendas which had fallen to his share when the great repartition of land had taken place. He operated also the largest dairy farm in the country, furnishing milk and butter and cheese to every charitable institution, orphans' home, insane asylum, reform school and work house in the country, and getting just twice the prices for them that any other dairy farm would have asked.[6]

However, Porter's Mexican themes were not all political by any means. She was intensely interested in all aspects of the Mexican scene. In "María Concepción," one of her most superb stories, she studies the elemental nature of the Mexican worker and his women. Juan is married to María Concepción, but he deserts her for another woman, María Rosa, and goes off to join the revolutionary armies, taking María Rosa with him. She becomes one of the *soldaderas*, the women who served the soldiers of the Revolution both as lovers and as the nearest thing to a supply corps the revolutionary armies ever had. When they return home, María Concepción kills her rival. When the police come to investigate, they are blanketed by the obdurate silence of the villagers and depart in frustration. Juan and María Concepción are reunited, and María Concepción takes on the care and raising of the baby which had been born to her dead rival. This story is a persuasive study of people who live close to the land and who are ruled by their own community traditions. As such the story is an example of a genuine, not a condescending, treatment of a primitivistic theme.

But Porter could also manage, with cheerful malice, a satire on the fake literary primitivism of her day. The story "That Tree" deals with an American newspaperman who has gone to Mexico City to make himself into a literary figure. In order to be properly "primitive" he equips himself with an Indian mistress, but he has a Midwestern schoolteacher wife who later comes down to join him—thus he must clear out his apartment. One night he takes his wife out dancing to a nightclub. Later in the evening, one of four quarreling generals gets to his feet and grabs for his gun. Immediately the Mexican girls on the dance floor, in a gesture which seems to "the journalist" to display a magnificently primitive instinct for self-preservation, swing their partners' backs toward the generals as shields. His wife simply dives under the table. This action strikes "the journalist" as "the most utterly humiliating moment of his whole, blighted life." Later he accuses her of having "instincts out of tune." She glares at him, and "when she tightened her mouth to bite her lip and say 'instincts,' she could make it sound like the most obscene word in the language."

It was in Mexico that Katherine Anne Porter developed what Givner calls "the rich superstructure of symbolism" which was to give a new dimension to the American short story. The recognition of her achievement led others to follow her to the source of her inspiration. She clearly was the nucleus of the American literary venture to postrevolutionary Mexico. It is doubtful, for example, whether the poet Hart Crane would have gone to Mexico City if the way had not been paved for him. Katherine Anne Porter, in fact, offered him a room in her house—a gesture that she was later to regret. By this time Crane was fully beset with his demons and well gone in alcoholism. Mexico, however, impressed him deeply, and some of his finest letters record his reactions to the land and people. The last poem he was to complete, and one of his best, "The Broken Tower," was written in Mexico. There also remain some beautiful fragments of an uncompleted poem on an Aztec theme,

"Xochipilli." But for a man in Hart Crane's desperate condition, Mexico, the country which has venerated death, was clearly not the place to go for a cure. On the way home, he jumped from the liner *Orizaba* and drowned.

But this tragedy did not diminish the lure of Mexico for American writers. The idea had become established that Mexico represented the nexus between indigenous and European America. The poet William Carlos Williams, who never forsook his other trade as a medical doctor, first entered Mexico with a patient in 1906. The Hispanic part of his heritage urged him to remain alert to cultural developments in Latin America. In 1925 he published his influential group of essays called *In the American Grain*. The Aztec civilization of Mexico remained for him the potent symbol of what was quintessentially American: "The New World is Montezuma or, since he was stoned to death in a parley, Guatemozin who had the city of Mexico leveled over him before he was taken." The poet Archibald MacLeish also came to Mexico searching for the origins of the American experience. On muleback he retraced the route that Cortez and his army had taken from Vera Cruz to the capital of the Aztecs, Tenochtitlán, now Mexico City. In his epic narrative poem *Conquistador,* he took on the persona of Bernal Díaz del Castillo, soldier in the army of Cortez, who had written a vivid account of the conquest of Mexico. For MacLeish, the encounter between Cortez and Montezuma was the most dramatic confrontation of European and indigenous America, and thus stood as an essential American myth. The novelist John Dos Passos also came to Mexico during this period. In his revolutionary interests he harkened back to the work of London, Reed, and Steffens. In fact, in *Nineteen Nineteen,* part of the *U.S.A.* trilogy, Dos Passos said of Reed that "Mexico taught him to write." In *The 42nd Parallel,* another volume in the trilogy, Mac, a former Wobbly, goes to Mexico and makes contact with members of the I.W.W. there. His faith in revolution is rekindled.

It is well acknowledged that the early twentieth century produced the greatest upsurge in modern American literature. This is the period that is called modernism in university classrooms. What is not generally acknowledged is the germinal role that Mexico played in the development of American modernism.

# 8

## Images of the Mexican in American Literature

Culturally the American Southwest has never been a static region. The continual interaction of two quite different cultures in the area, whatever else it might have done, has insured the Southwest against monotony. The word *interaction* can carry the connotation of conflict, and in terms of the history of the region, that meaning is certainly not unwarranted. But this interaction has taken a number of forms, and not the least of them has been the function of the Southwest as a conduit through which the potent influences of Latin American culture have made their way into the United States. A case in point is the manner in which the more recent Chicano writers have adopted and modified literary techniques of the brilliant new novelists of South America and Mexico. In the course of this absorption, Chicano literature, aside from its own strongly original impulses, has incorporated and fused North American and Latin American literary traditions. But I am getting well ahead of my story. The essential point being made is that the interaction of Latin American and North American cultures throughout a huge area of the United States has been continual, unavoidable, sometimes stressful, but always exciting. That the literature of the United States has felt the continued influence of Mexico, often through the medium of the Southwest, is a matter of record. The pressures of Mexican and Southwestern influences upon North American culture have been continually exerted since the early decades of the nineteenth century, and American writers have had to react to them in one way or another.

It is certainly true that the early American writers on the Hispanic Southwest had very little give to them. Most of these people were not writers in the way that we think of the profession of writing today. Few of them were literary artists, and few of them did anything to damage their amateur standing. They were, on the whole, mountain men, soldiers, government officials, newspaper people off the beaten track, or just travelers and adventurers. Nevertheless, the reports they produced are interesting and significant, perhaps the more so because those who wrote them were broadly representative of the people of their times.

The United States in the 1830s and 1840s, the period in which North Americans and Mexicans first collided in the Southwest, was a considerably more homogeneous nation than it is today. It was prevailingly rural, Protestant, and Anglo-Saxon. As it pushed westward, it removed itself increasingly from the cultural influences of Europe. It became quite conscious of being different and new, but whatever benefits this newness bestowed upon it were accompanied by a certain rawness and provincialism. It was a period between a successful revolution and a devastating civil war. There was a widespread optimism and not a little naiveté. Faith in continual progress through the new science and technology ran high. The sinister strain was black slavery in the South—"the bell tolling in the night," as Jefferson put it. Black slavery entered upon the Mexican scene as Anglo-Americans brought their slaves with them into a Texas under Mexican rule. Incidentally, the fact that approximately 80 percent of the white Americans who entered Texas were from the American South influenced racial attitudes toward darker people not only in Texas but also in New Mexico and Arizona, where many Texans later migrated. This, then, was the scene from which the early borderland reports emanated. These chronicles written by North American writers inevitably included reactions to Mexican society.

As mentioned above, Americans of the period were beginning their long infatuation with science and technology. In itself this interest is not to be disparaged, and it has clearly produced results. However, as American writers such as Hawthorne have pointed out, the abstractions of science cannot replace humanitarian concerns. But in this period there was a tendency to equate human well-being and progress almost exclusively with scientific advancement. People in such a frame of mind might be expected to look down upon a society less concerned with matters of

science. A number of the borderland chroniclers took Mexico to task for
its lack of scientific advancement. Typical of holders of this attitude was
George Wilkins Kendall, a journalist who had founded the *New Orleans
Picayune* and had traveled a good deal in the borderlands area. In an
account of his experiences in Mexico he wrote:

> Strange that with a country as fair as any upon the face of the earth,
> abounding in every species of soil and climate, fruit and mineral, the Mexi-
> cans will not profit from the lessons and adopt the systems of their Saxon
> neighbors. They pertinaciously cling to the customs of their forefathers, and
> are becoming every year more and more impoverished—in short they are
> morally, physically, and intellectually distanced in the great race of improve-
> ment which is run in almost every other quarter of the earth. Give them but
> tortillas, frijoles, and chile colorado to supply their animal wants for the day,
> and seven-tenths of the Mexicans are satisfied; and so they will continue to
> be until the race becomes extinct or amalgamated with Anglo-Saxon stock;
> for no political change, no revolution can uproot that inherent indolence
> and antipathy to change, which in this age of improvement and advance-
> ment must sooner or later work their ruin and downfall. In these wonder-
> working days of steam, to stand still is to retrograde.[1]

Allusion has already been made to racial attitudes prevalent in the
Southwest during this period. What is somewhat surprising to a modern
reader is the unabashed way in which some of the borderland chroniclers
expressed their racial antipathies. A respectable San Francisco periodical
included a story by a writer who described one of his characters as being
"a ragged, dirty Mexican, whose matted hair was the model of a cactus
fence, whose tattered blanket served to make more evident his nakedness, an unmistakable, unredeemed 'greaser.' "[2]

In attempting to cope with or at least make an assessment of a culture
which seemed so radically different from their own, the North Americans
in the frontier region of the Southwest found themselves faced with a
dilemma. It was all very well to excoriate an illiterate, mestizo peasantry,
but how to deal with the Mexican aristocracy, whose life of elegant
leisure impressed them in spite of themselves? One way to handle this
was to think of the classes as being really two different peoples. An
arbitrary and false distinction was set up between *Spaniard* and *Mexican*,
the one being the landed aristocrat, the other being the peon who
worked for him or did other menial kinds of labor. In this, the *criollo* era in
Mexican history, there hardly existed a middle class in Mexico, with the
exception of the rancheros of northern Mexico— who were something
of a breed apart. One of a number of examples of the arbitrary distinction

between *Spaniard* and *Mexican* can be found in the writings of John Russell Bartlett, a U.S. boundary commissioner who worked in the Southwest during the 1840s and 1850s. Though he had a general disdain for Mexicans as a whole, he responded respectfully and appreciatively to the wealthy Mexicans who entertained him in El Paso. The following passage can be found in his lengthy memoirs:

> There are a few respectable old Spanish families in El Paso, who possess much intelligence, as well as that elegance and dignity of manner which characterized their ancestors. . . . A vast gulf intervenes between these Castilians and the masses, who are a mixed breed, possessing none of the virtue of their European ancestors, but all their vices, with those of the aborigines superadded.[3]

This class and race distinction, established in the minds of early North Americans in the borderlands, was to be a heritage bequeathed to later generations and to be a source of friction extending into the twentieth century, a situation which will be examined later.

One could generalize by saying that the still provincial and ethnocentric United States of the mid nineteenth century reacted negatively to a complex society which it seemed unable or unwilling to understand. An indication of this confused reaction is that the writers of the border chronicles were capable of ascribing contradictory characteristics to the Mexicans. They were on the one hand rapacious, thievish, and murderous, and on the other, superstitiously religious, docile, and cowardly. The still Puritan mind recoiled from what was felt to be a pervasive Mexican sensuality, and literally hundreds of pages were devoted to the superstitious, paganistic, and corrupt Roman Catholic Church in Mexico.

There is one large exception to the negative report on Mexico by North American writers of the mid nineteenth century. The writers of New England were in several ways against the grain in terms of general American thought and feeling during this period. In their passionate opposition to slavery, they did not share in that racism which the South had imported to a good deal of the West. Furthermore, New England did not support the concept of manifest destiny, in which so much of the country was feverishly caught up. In fact, the New England intellectuals and writers opposed the Mexican-American War. They conceived of it as an imperialistic adventure, and they suspected the government of President James Polk, a Southerner, of conniving to extend slavery into the western territories. In his ode to W. H. Channing, Ralph Waldo Emerson wrote: "Behold the famous States / Harrying Mexico / With rifle and with knife."[4] The pawky Hosea Bigelow, created by James Russell Lowell, amused readers of the *Boston Courier* with his sharp sallies against slavery and the Mexican War delivered in the tart dialect of rural New England. Henry David Thoreau, famous for having gone to jail rather than pay taxes in support of the Mexican War, inveighed against the war in his essay "Civil Disobedience." The poet, essayist, and journalist William Cullen Bryant was one of the first of the American writers to be actively interested in Latin American culture. He toured through the Caribbean and Mexico, and has left journals and essays in which he recorded his observations on those regions. In Mexico, he became a friend and strong admirer of Benito Juárez. He noted that not only Juárez, but Vice President Ramirez and the distinguished historian and literary man Ignacio Altamirano, to whom he had been introduced, were full-blooded Indians. His comment upon this circumstance stands in marked contrast with the racist harangues of the borderland chroniclers. "Many of these descendents of the people subdued by Cortez," wrote Bryant, "are men of cultivated minds and engaging manners. The greatest part of the works of art in the galleries of which I have spoken [Mexican Academy of Arts] are from their hands."[5]

As the nineteenth century moved from its middle to its later years, other North American voices were heard on the subject of Mexico and the Hispanic Southwest. Walt Whitman, whose poetic voice still rings powerfully among us, discovered his real position later in life. As a young reporter for the *Brooklyn Eagle*, he joined in the enthusiasm for manifest destiny and its mystique of western expansionism—even though it be at the expense of a neighbor. In his exhortations, he conjured up some of the old stereotypes that we have been dealing with. However, in 1883, Whitman received a letter from the city fathers of Santa Fe, New Mexico, in which he was asked to provide a poem in honor of the occasion of the three hundred and thirty-third anniversary of the founding of the city. Instead of sending a poem, Whitman sent a letter to "Messrs. Griffin, Martinez, Prince and other Gentlemen at Santa Fe." After asserting that Americans generally have allowed themselves to be "impress'd by New England writers and schoolmasters" into thinking that American character derives from England alone, he states that such a concept is "a very great mistake." America he says, derives its strength from several different sources, and "to that composite American identity of the future, Spanish character will supply some of the most needed parts." At this point, Whitman deals a strong blow to the famous "black legend" (*la leyenda negra*) with which both British and North American writers have painted Spain and her cultural extensions in the Americas.

> It is time to dismiss utterly the illusion-compound, half raw-head-and-bloody bones and half Mysteries of Udolpho, inherited from the English writers of the past 200 years. It is time to realize—for it is certainly true—that there will not be found any more cruelty, tyranny, superstition, etc. in the *resume* of past Spanish history than in the corresponding *resume* of Anglo-Norman history. Nay, I think there will not be found so much.[6]

Whitman then turns his attention to the coming cultural contributions of the Hispanic Southwest. True to the prophetic element in his nature, he foresees a development that we now can recognize as the flowering of Chicano culture.

> As to the Spanish stock of our Southwest, it is certain to me that we do not begin to appreciate the splendor and sterling value of its race element. Who knows but that element, like the course of some subterranean river, dipping invisibly for a hundred or two years, is now to emerge in broadest flow and permanent action?[7]

Whitman's letter was a harbinger of changing attitudes toward Mexico and the Hispanic Southwest. But the first evidence of this change was to take a rather special form. Perhaps it was the clanging new industrialism of what Mark Twain dubbed the Gilded Age that made people long for quieter and more serene times. At any rate there arose in the Southwest, particularly in California, a literature that was in marked contrast with the cocky borderland chronicles of earlier in the century. Instead of being an object of derogation, the Hispanic tradition in the Southwest now came to be looked upon as something to be venerated. The new people pouring into California suddenly discovered that, raw as they might be, they had a tradition there for the taking: an ancient, dignified, and romantic one. Thus began what came to be known as the California idyll in American letters. Gallant caballeros and beautiful senoritas, enticingly veiled in black mantillas—with the mission churches in the background—began to people a literature that became quickly and immensely popular. Here was a literary vein with much gold in it, and it was thoroughly worked by such writers as Joaquin Miller, Mark Twain, Helen Hunt Jackson, Gertrude Atherton, Charles Warren Stoddard, and Bret Harte. Harte, for example, gives the following nostalgic account of his first visit to San Francisco:

I recall . . . my wanderings through the Spanish Quarter, where three centuries of quaint customs, speech, and dress were still preserved; where the
proverbs of Sancho Panza were still spoken in the language of Cervantes,
and the high-flown illusions of the La Manchian knight were still a part of
the Spanish Californian Hidalgo's dream.[8]

Carey McWilliams in *North from Mexico* makes much the same point.
Thus a fantasy heritage, fostered by a literary movement, was made to
substitute for the reality of the Mexican presence in California, and the
distinctions which this heritage made were used to justify such policies as
segregation and exclusion.

But the purveyors of the California idyll were soon displaced by writers
who were prepared to treat Mexico seriously. There were reasons for this
change in attitude. The Civil War was a watershed period in American
life. Until the war, the United States was largely the homogeneous nation
described earlier: rural, Protestant, and Anglo-Saxon. With the war there
came the sudden need for munitions. It was the North that was able to
rapidly develop an industrial base, a fact which largely accounts for its
victory. After the conflict, factories established to produce munitions
were converted to peacetime uses. The age of heavy industry was upon
us, with immense social and cultural consequences. Young people in
droves escaped the hard life of the country for what was to prove an
equally hard life in the factory. Long-standing country traditions were left
behind. At the same time Europe opened its floodgates of emigration to
feed the new industrialism in America. Languages, customs, and traditions of the Old World were abandoned by many immigrants. The word
*alienation* came into the American vocabulary. The result of all these
uprooting forces was a chastened mood among American writers. Under
the new and bewildering conditions, they began to look with something
like envy upon a nation to the south which had managed to preserve a
culture in depth.

This being the case, it is not really surprising that a large number of
modern North American writers with national and international reputa-
tions have written seriously about Mexico. A partial list would include
Stephen Crane, Jack London, Sherwood Anderson, Carl Sandburg, Willa
Cather, Ernest Hemingway, John Steinbeck, John Dos Passos, Robinson
Jeffers, Archibald MacLeish, William Carlos Williams, Katherine Anne
Porter, Henry Miller, Wright Morris, Allen Ginsberg, Gregory Corso,
Lawrence Ferlinghetti, Joseph Wood Krutch, and Saul Bellow.

It is curious and no doubt significant that the emergent, multicultural

United States of the twentieth century should be admiring in Mexico the very things that the nineteenth-century North American writers criticized so vehemently. The faith in automatic progress through science having vanished, the modern American writer is hardly likely to take the Mexican to task for being unprogressive, as did George Wilkins Kendall. To the contrary, the Mexican is now being praised as being closer to the essential rhythms of life. Instead of being declared sexually immoral, the Mexican is now seen as happily free of puritanical "hangups" and more realistic in terms of the biological functions of humanity. The richness, drama, and intensity of Mexico's religious life, formerly declared superstitious and paganistic, is now being compared with the paleness and absence of religious forms in the United States—a point notably made by Willa Cather in *Death Comes for the Archbishop* and in other of her writings.

The racism so prominent in the early writings has given way to an interest in the Mexican mestizo as a repository of two powerful heritages. Perhaps the turning point on this subject, as on a number of others, came in a book now largely forgotten but once very popular, Charles M. Flandrau's *Viva Mexico!* (1910). Flandrau's tone might be a bit patronizing, but the admiration is there. "In its way," he writes, "the mixture of Spaniard and tropical Indian—which was the original recipe for making the contemporary Mexican—is physically a pleasing one. It isn't our way, but one doesn't after a while find it less attractive for that."[9] In Jack London's story "The Mexican," Felipe Rivera, the protagonist, becomes a boxer in California in order to raise money for the cause of the Mexican Revolution. He represents the coming people of Mexico, the men of the earth, and his fierce stoic strength is credited to the fact that he draws his blood from two strong and warlike races.

Yet with all this aroused interest and goodwill in the portrayal of the Mexican by modern American writers, there still has been, no doubt unintentionally, a falling into stereotype. Part of this has to do with the infatuation of American writers with primitivism, a reaction against what has seemed to be a shallow, machine-run, "plastic" society in the United States. Writers such as Steinbeck and Hemingway have liked their Mexicans and Spaniards best when they can be shown as primitive, elemental, close to the earth. No doubt Steinbeck loved his "paisanos," and he portrayed them most affectionately. As devil-may-care livers for the day—take, for example, Danny and his friends in *Tortilla Flat*—they seem to fill an inner need for their creator. They are active upbraiders of all that is schedulized, punctualized, and appointment-bound in Anglo-

American life. Yet for all their animation they amount to a reduction to stereotype of members of a complex culture.

Katherine Anne Porter has recognized the pseudoprimitivistic element in some American writing and has been able, in a cheerfully malicious manner, to satirize it. In the story "That Tree," Porter's protagonist is an American journalist who goes to Mexico with the design of converting himself into a primitivistic writer. In the course of his efforts, he only succeeds in making himself ridiculous. Yet when Porter herself turned to the elemental aspects of Mexican rural life, she came up with the beautifully rendered "María Concepción."

Modern American writers are, therefore, capable of treating Mexico realistically as well as appreciatively. Another example of this can be found in Joseph Wood Krutch's book *The Forgotten Peninsula,* in which the author describes the individualism and style that people have been able to maintain even in the remote communities of Baja California. In *The Milagro Beanfield War* and his other novels of northern New Mexico, John Nichols may occasionally lapse into quaintness, but on the whole his Hispanos are drawn robustly and, to bring in a welcome element, with a rich sense of humor.

While the image of the Mexican in the literature of the United States has been undergoing radical transformations in the twentieth century, it has also been passing into the hands of a new group of artists. In terms of the Hispanic Southwest, the Chicano writers have been providing the most important angle of vision and the one that had heretofore been lacking: the point of view from within the culture itself. Whether in the future this will prove to be the only viable angle of vision remains to be seen. Though the question lies beyond the scope of this paper, it can at least be said that the Chicano writers, who are revivifying the literature of the Southwest, have by their contributions allowed for a double view of the Chicano in American literature, the view from without and the view from within.

# 9

## Del Rancho al Campo:
### *The Ranch and Farm in the Literature of the Southwest*

The earliest cattle ranches in the Southwest had endless space in which to work. They were able, therefore, to settle into the desert areas almost as if they were natural features of the terrain. The ranch and the techniques of cattle raising in the Southwest were in fact first developed by the Mexicans, beginning in Spanish colonial times. The Anglo-Americans, upon penetrating the region, learned these techniques from the Mexicans, and the great western cattle spread was born. These developments were traced by novelist Tom Lea in the history of one such spread, *The King Ranch*.

> The hacienda's work developed a picturesque and unprecedented type of New World herdsman: the vaquero. It was this vaquero of Mexico who invented a technique for the horseback handling of half-wild cattle on an open range. He became adept at tossing a coiled rawhide rope he made with a sliding noose. He sat a saddle with a pummel he designed and built as a sturdy snubbing post for his rope, to hold what he caught. He rode a strong-legged tender-mouthed pony he trained for the work of herding and roping. He used the branding iron derived from Spain to burn the mark of ownership into an animal's living hide.[1]

In the course of this apprenticeship, the Anglo-Americans not only absorbed the language of the trade from their Mexican teachers; they also acquired from them the needed equipment. As Edward Larocque

Tinker tells us in *The Horsemen of the Americas and the Literature They Inspired:*

> The North Americans established ranches of their own and stocked them from the great unbranded herds. They needed cowboys to take care of them, but the young men from the Atlantic coast knew nothing of how to manage huge numbers of wild, fierce long-horns roaming an unfenced continent. They had to learn how to ride herd from the Mexican vaquero, how to break a bronco, and to use riatas and branding irons. They adopted his entire equipment—the ring bit, that was copied by the Spaniards from the Moors and is still in use in parts of the Southwest, and the stock saddle which is merely a slightly modified form of the Conquistadores', with a horn added for roping. Even the cowboys' workaday vocabulary is generously peppered, in the Southwest, with Spanish words.[2]

This vocabulary absorption from one language into another is a sure expression of the interlocking nature of the two cultures.

The traditional Mexican cattle ranches in the Sonoran desert were marvels of adaptation to the desert region. In *Pony Tracks, Sketches of Pioneer Life,* written at the end of the nineteenth century, the western painter Frederic Remington describes one such ranch, the hacienda San José de Bavicora. The vaqueros to Remington were men "untainted by the enfeebling influences of luxury and modern life." He saw these hard-riding vaqueros of northern Mexico as splendid examples of adaptation to terrain and of freedom and virility.

That such adaptation still exists on the Sonoran ranch is a central theme in Tom Lea's novel *Wonderful Country,* in which he describes the character and way of life of a Sonoran ranchero, Don Santiago Santos. Don Santiago says of himself:

> We Santos . . . we live where we belong, I think. We have lived in the Bavinuchi since the times of the King Carlos III. He granted us the land. A Santos was Marqués of Sonora. We do not produce any *Marqueses* in these times, nor any damned politicians either. . . . We Santos produce *rancheros.* I wish there were more of us. By the time there is fuzz on our cheeks we have learned the music of the bull pens, we know horses and firearms and these sierras.[3]

Don Santiago Santos is a representative of a desert-bred class of men who are products of the vast northern states of Mexico such as Sonora, Chihuahua, Coahuila, and Durango. The desert made them tough, resourceful, and self-reliant. Unlike the owners of the great haciendas to the south of them, who lounged in their town houses in Mexico City or

Paris while the overseers ran the hacienda, and the peons, like medieval serfs, did the grueling work, the rancheros of the north were owners and operators of their often small ranchos. They worked beside their vaqueros—and represented a kind of independent middle class.

It was no coincidence that the *norteños*, the men from the North, started, won, and ruled the great revolution that began in 1910 and continued into the early 1920s, and changed Mexico radically. When the dictator Porfirio Díaz sent his army north to squelch them, the vaqueros swept out of the desert and cracked that army wide open. Porfirio Díaz fled to France. The leaders of the Revolution—Madero, Villa, Carranza, Obregón, and Calles—were all *norteños*. The workings of the Sonoran ranch which produced this type of man are still more adaptation than exploitation. The features of the desert terrain are adapted to rather than changed. The Mexican influence is still felt in some of the American ranches close to the border. Such a ranch is the central locale of the novel *The Black Bull*, by Frank Goodwyn. Anglo and Mexican ranch hands not only work on intimate terms with each other but also, in important ways, share a common culture.

Yet by the late nineteenth and early twentieth centuries conditions of ranch life in the Southwest had begun to change. In the novel *The Sea of Grass* by Conrad Richter (1936), Colonel Jim Brewster, old-time rancher and autocrat, tries vainly to stem the encroachment of homesteaders, "nesters," on the vast land he claims. The open range with its adaptive nature is being closed in, and the land is being put to other uses.

Yet the desire for wilderness and the open range may exist as a sort of anachronistic conditioning in the heart of the modern cowboy. One of this dwindling breed is Jack Burns in Edward Abbey's novel *The Brave Cowboy* (1972). Burns tries to flee neon-lighted Albuquerque into a life on the open range but discovers that such a life no longer exists. Whatever ranching still continues is hemmed in, motorized, and mechanized.

Jack Burns at least has the virtues, if not the functions, of the earlier breed. Hud, in Larry McMurty's novel *Horseman Pass By* (1961), upon which the motion picture *Hud* was based, represents a perversion of the mythic cowboy hero. Hud is a boozer, skirt chaser, schemer, and finally murderer. The town and the indulgences it offers to Hud are not far from the ranch.

The history of desert farming in the Southwest has some similarity to that of ranching, and the literatures that deal with them share things in common. The change that occurred in agriculture was from the small subsistence farming practiced by the Pueblo Indians and Mexicans to the large commercial farming characteristic of the Anglo-Americans. Novelist Harvey Fergusson in his cultural history *Rio Grande* notes the different attitudes toward the land of the "paisanos" of the small communities in New Mexico and the "American farmer of the Anglo-Saxon breed." The former is "a lover of the earth who asks nothing better than to live his whole life on one patch of soil, scratching it for a living, laying his bones in it at last." The latter "does not cherish the earth, he loves to conquer it. Always he tends to exhaust the soil and move on. . . . His interest is always in a 'money crop.'"

The Hispanic farmers in Frank Waters's *People of the Valley* are depicted as adapting themselves to the land and making modest demands of it. They resist the plan, conceived by Anglo authorities, to build a large dam that would flood a number of traditional Mexican homes and farming areas but would allow for large-scale, profitable farming. The "people of the valley" are unmoved by the argument that the sacrifice of a traditional way of life will in the long run make them into prosperous farmers.

In his racy novel *The Milagro Beanfield War,* John Nichols uses the planned building of a dam in New Mexico as the center of conflict. The realization of expansion plans for a tourist and recreational area in the small community of Milagro in northern New Mexico depends upon the erection of the Indian Creek Dam, which would preempt all the neighboring water. This plan pits developer Ladd Devine III, backed by the governor of the state and the establishment generally, against Joe Mondragon and his fellow Hispanic farmers. By persistent courage, shrewd maneuvers, and guerrilla tactics, the poor farmers and their sympathizers defeat Devine and the forces arrayed behind him. The governor of the state, realizing that there will not be the easy victory that he has expected, and fearing that the Chicano militants will get wind of the Milagro beanfield war and join forces with Mondragon, backs away from his support of Ladd Devine.

Ranching and farming and the tensions between the two in New Mexico provide an important theme in the novel *Bless Me, Ultima* by Rudolfo Anaya. The narrator of the novel is a young boy, Tony Márez, who feels within himself the conflict of two traditions, traditions which in fact have been in conflict throughout the West. His father's people are vaqueros from the llanos (plains), dating back to the unfenced era when the cattle were driven over huge distances. His mother comes from a family of farmers, stable people, loving workers of the soil. Tony is torn between his father's ideal of freedom and his mother's of stability and piety. In her effort to influence him, his mother sends Tony during the summers to work on the farms of her brothers. There he experiences the deep affinity felt by the Hispanic farmer of New Mexico for the soil that he works. Tony is an excellent student at school and appears to be headed toward the intellectual life, which could in fact resolve his conflict.

The small farm of New Mexico was not typical of farming endeavors in the Southwest. The Anglo-American farmer, as indicated above, sought the big-money crop, which presupposed a largeness of operation. But in order to bring in the big-money crop, it was often necessary to superimpose artificial structures on the land. The San Joaquin Valley of southern California was reclaimed from the desert by irrigation, and railroads were needed to move the crop to market. Historically there has been conflict between the farmers of the valley and the powerful railroad company upon which they became dependent. An actual case of a clash between them was fictionalized by Frank Norris in his novel *The Octopus,* in which a "ranchers league" of wheat farmers engaged in a pitched battle with "goon squads" hired by the railroad. While men fought over it, the wheat itself appeared in *The Octopus* as a powerful natural force indifferent to the puny affairs of men.

The great agricultural spreads of the Southwest, unlike the agriculture engaged in by Indian or Mexican farmers on their small plots of land, cannot be family run. An outside work force is needed, and this has been provided in many cases by migrant laborers, many of them Mexicans or Mexican-Americans. The woes of these often exploited people have produced what might be considered a subgenre in the literature of the Southwest. There has even been a special form of theater which has arisen to dramatize the plight of the Mexican and Mexican-American agricultural workers in the Southwest. This theater has come to be known as the Teatro Campesino (Peasants' Theater). It had its origin in the fields of Delano, California, where César Chávez's United Farm Workers organized a strike against the grape growers in the 1960s. The founder of the Teatro Campesino was the director Luis Miguel Valdez, and the early skits or *actos,* dramatizing the issues of the strike, were often performed in the backs of open trucks which acted as moving stages. The early, improvised *actos* later grew into established repertoires and branched into other areas of Chicano social concerns. There are now *teatros* throughout the Southwest, but the beginnings of this movement in the Teatro Campesino are not lost sight of.

Not unexpectedly, a number of the novels and short stories which comprise the body of work of Chicano literature devote themselves to the lives of agricultural workers. One of the best of these, written entirely in

Spanish, is *Peregrinos de Aztlán* (Pilgrims of Aztlán) by Miguel Méndez. The word *Aztlán* refers to the legendary original home of the Aztecs, which is presumed to have been in northwest Mexico. It means different things to different groups of Chicanos, but its common denominator of meaning is the area of the Southwest where the Chicanos live and make their presence felt. Méndez's novel traces the movement of Mexican undocumented workers across the infernal deserts of Arizona to the cotton fields, fruit orchards, or vineyards of California and Arizona. "Wetbacks" and Chicano workers are compared with their Anglo employers and other authority figures. The latter tend to run to a type: red-faced, aseptic puritans who, on the one hand, are churchgoers and constant Bible readers and, on the other, are exploiters of their Mexican and Chicano workers.

As an overview, it could be said that both ranching and farming in the desert regions of the Southwest have gone through successive phases, moving from an initial adaptation to the desert environment to various forms of artificial "improvement" upon that environment. The literary record reflects these changes and suggests that later "improvements" might have entailed losses to be reckoned not only in environmental but also in human terms.

# 10

## Through the Southwest—By Road, Rail, and Waterway

Roads, railways, and canals, however conducive they may have been to the productivity of the Southwest, are also superstructures placed upon the desert floor that have increasingly put a strain upon the ecology of the region. The first main highway of travel in the Southwest was no more than a beaten path through plains, mountains, and deserts. The Santa Fe Trail was the primordial or ur road of the region, and the literature that grew up around it is rich and extensive. It includes *Prose Poems and Sketches* (1834) by Albert Pike, the first Southwestern short stories in English, and a number of narratives such as Josiah Webb's *Adventures in the Santa Fe Trade 1844–1847* (1931), Lewis H. Garrard's *Wah-To-Yah and the Taos Trail* (1850), Susan Shelby Magoffin's *Down the Santa Fe Trail and into Mexico* (1926), and Josiah Gregg's *Commerce of the Prairies* (1851). This literature gives a number of (mainly unwitting) examples of American ethnocentricity in dealing with the complex culture of Mexico, and it also indicates that even before the Mexican-American War the New Mexico territory had, because of trade along the Santa Fe Trail, become an economic appendage of the United States. The trail started the process of change by which the Southwest ceased to be a preindustrial Indian and Hispanic area and began to become a commercialized and technologized section of the United States.

Many of the early trails in the Southwest became the later roads and highways. As such they can serve not only as examples but also as symbols of the change from one way of life to another. In the Chicano novel *Bless Me, Ultima* by Rudolfo Anaya, Gabriel Márez, the father of the narrator, works as a road builder and repairer in rural New Mexico. As a young man he had been a vaquero. He could still remember when ranching was carried on in great stretches of open country. The work provided a living for his family, but it marked his confinement and degradation, and he hated it. At home Gabriel was sullen and did a good deal of solitary drinking.

In contrast with the road as symbol of confinement in *Bless Me, Ultima,* Highway 66 in John Steinbeck's *The Grapes of Wrath* was the avenue of escape from the dust bowl for the "Okies." A quarter of a million people and fifty thousand old cars were in full flight across the deserts of the Southwest. "Where did the courage come from?" is a refrain in the novel.

From yet another point of view, many of the roads in the Southwest seemed to Edward Abbey to be enemies of conservation. In *Desert Solitaire,* he maintained that roads should be eliminated from the national parks. They were agencies of the commercialism of the parks and were destroying them. In *The Monkey Wrench Gang,* the eco-raiders express their disgust at a modern highway under construction in Utah at the expense of many trees and other natural features. The old road is perfectly serviceable. It would simply take the traveler a bit longer to reach a destination.

Of the various superstructures laid upon the desert, the railroad was the most dramatic and historic. It radically changed life in the Southwest. The arrival of the Southern Pacific railroad at Tucson in 1880, for example, wrought a radical transformation upon the town. Before that, Tucson was commercially and culturally appended to the Mexican state of Sonora. Whatever merchandise, equipment, or entertainment Tucson could come by arrived by wagon from Mexico. It was in essence a Mexican community. The railroad provided a nexus with the rest of the country, and the gringo-ization of Tucson rapidly followed.

The transformation caused by the railroad became an important theme in the literature of the Southwest. In *Great River,* his splendid cultural history of the Rio Grande and the countryside along its banks, Paul Horgan makes clear that the advent of the railroad destroyed the old freedom of the cowboys.

The main trunk lines of the railroads ran east to west across the continent; but soon feeder lines were built—sometimes following the flat terrain of the old trails—and machine transportation reached nearer and nearer to the great ranches of the border where the whole cattle industry had had its beginnings. The Missouri, Kansas, and Texas Railroad was the great Texas cattle line. It tapped the Rio Grande brush country ranges. The Atchison, Topeka, and Santa Fe main line crossed New Mexico and a branch line ran from Belen on the Rio Grande all the way down the valley to El Paso. The Texas and Pacific reached eastward from San Diego to El Paso in 1877, and bridges now came back to the Rio Grande to stay. The whole river empire was soon tied to the rest of the nation by rails. When packing houses were established at Kansas City, Fort Worth and other Southwestern cities, the final pattern of the organized beef cattle industry was realized. In it there was little room for the figure, the temperament, of the original cowboy with his individual lordship over great unimpeded distances and his need of freedom as he defined it. His cow camp literature recorded yet another stage—the last—of his history. "The cowboy has left the country," he could sing, "and the campfire has gone out."[1]

Stephen Crane's story "The Bride Comes to Yellow Sky" reveals a point of change in the life of a small southwest Texas town and the old West which it represents. Jack Potter, the town's marshal, does not recognize the extent to which the train on which he is riding back to town—and admires lavishly—and the bride he is bringing with him represent an end to the era in which he reigned. Harvey Fergusson in his trilogy of novels *Followers of the Sun* dramatizes the way in which the advent of the railroad to New Mexico brought in the ascendancy of the incoming Anglos and wiped out the old Mexican patriarchs and their haciendas.

The advent of the railroads resulted in mining, that traditional occupation in the deserts of the Southwest dating back to Spanish colonial times, taking a new lease on life. This point is emphatically made in the novel *The Blue Chip* by Ysabel Rennie, whose plot centers around the development of an Arizona copper mine. At one point the narrator says, "The opening of the Jerico short line was high water mark with us. . . . With the coming of the railroad, the Blue Chip began to make money."

In agriculture, too, the railroads brought great changes. They made large-scale farming possible in the Southwest. Sometimes, particularly in the earlier period, the railroad companies misused their immense power at the expense of the farmers who had to depend upon them to bring their produce to market. Also, the railroads held large land options in the Southwest, and railroad-owned land was used by farmers and ranchers at sufferance. These circumstances sometimes became occasions of severe conflict, as was dramatized by Frank Norris in the novel *The Octopus*.

When the railroad called in its land options, violating promises it had made to wheat farmers in the San Joaquin Valley, and also arbitrarily raised freight rates, a pitched battle ensued between "the ranchers league" and agents of the railroad. The wheat farmers were bloodily defeated by "the octopus."

The desert areas were to see the railroad used in another kind of combat. Pancho Villa, in the great Mexican Revolution of 1910–1921, learned to use the railroad as a powerful improvised weapon, rolling troops across the desert—they would suddenly appear, to the consternation of his enemies—and later ripping up tracks when they could be of use to those who opposed him. Villa's creative use of the railroad as an instrument of war across the deserts of Chihuahua and Durango has been described in Paul Horgan's *Great River* and in Haldeen Braddy's biography of Villa, *Cock of the Walk.* In a memorable passage in her biography of Katherine Ann Porter, Joan Givner describes the young writer taking the train along Villa's old routes, shortly after the fighting had stopped. The desolated countryside with its haciendas in ruin and the bullet-scarred desert towns made a profound impression on the American writer who was to use Mexico so effectively as a locale for her short stories.

The great changes that have been brought about in the desert environment would not have been possible had it not been for the artificial introduction of water. The use of irrigation in the deserts of the Southwest dates back to the earliest of the Pueblo Indian cultures. Paul Horgan tells us that water was considered sacred by the peoples of these cultures and that certain springs became shrines. Therefore, when these people felt that they must manipulate water for agricultural purposes, they did so with the greatest care, so that the irrigation canals would not seem to be a human defilement but, rather, extensions of nature. They were made to appear to be little rivers melded into the landscape.

The early Mexican inhabitants of the region seem to have taken over this sense of fitting the irrigation ditches to the landscape, and to this day the *acequias* wander unobtrusively through the fields and even along the streets of small New Mexican communities. The *acequia madre,* the main artery which supplies water to the smaller canals, becomes a principal feature of such villages and provides a locale for novels and short stories dealing with New Mexico. In Frank Waters's *The People of the Valley,* the *acequias* were to be inundated by the water collected behind a proposed dam. This submerging of a traditional way of life brought strong opposition from the local people.

The irrigation practiced by the wheat farmers in Frank Norris's *The Octopus* is done on the grand commercial scale. The great irrigation ditch on one of the principal ranches, Los Muertos, is a central feature of the landscape. Another, temporarily dried-up, canal is large enough to serve as a trench for the "ranchers league" as, heavily armed, it takes battle positions and awaits the arrival of the agents of the Pacific and Southern Railroad, for which one might read the Southern Pacific.

Edward Abbey, highly conservation minded, makes a distinction between different types of irrigation. In *The Monkey Wrench Gang*, Doc Sarvis, respectable doctor turned eco-raider, curses large irrigation projects which serve to drain the water resources of the desert in support of big agricultural projects which are not needed and which the desert cannot sustain. But in *Desert Solitaire* Abbey praises the old-time, self-sustained Mormon communities which fit into but do not destroy the Utah desert. But these communities are on the way out. As Abbey put it:

> Subsequently swamped by the new American mode, by industrialism, commercialism, urbanism, rugged and ragged individualism, the old Mormon communities are now disappearing. But in such small towns as Moab, Kanab, Boulder and Escalante we can still see the handsome homes of hand-carved, sandstone blocks, the quiet streets lined with irrigation ditches and giant cottonwoods, the children riding their horses, which remind us on the downside of the twentieth century of what life must have been like in the nineteenth.[2]

Abbey talks as though it were already too late, in terms of the fragile nature of the desert ecology, which people like the writer and savant of the desert Joseph Wood Krutch have found unique. And certainly Abbey's pessimism is not to be lightly disregarded. But the notion of environmental protection in this country, while it goes back to the period of Theodore Roosevelt and before, gained real momentum only in comparatively recent times. This momentum is not getting the official encouragement that it used to. Therefore, it is all the more the task of humanists and scientists, working together, to maintain public interest in ecology, conservationism, and environmental protection. If a sense of responsibility toward the environment can be instilled as a permanent part of the public consciousness, then perhaps a somewhat gentle side, in Abbey's sense of those words, can be given to the century which is coming upon us.

# 11

## Miguel Méndez, the Voice in Spanish of the Borderlands

Miguel Méndez is without doubt an impressive man. There is about him the stalwartness that comes from early years spent as a day laborer in the state of Sonora, Mexico, where he grew up. That northern state is famous for producing a special breed, the *norteños* (men from the north), noted for their spirit of independence and their openness. There is not about them the elaborateness cultivated by Latin Americans in some other areas. They are a spacious people.

Many of the shops in Hermosillo, capital of the state of Sonora, are devoted to the sale of saddles and leather goods, articles which remind one that much of Sonora is still ranch country, and indeed in Sonora one breathes an air of openness that makes one think of the cattle kingdoms which once characterized the West in the United States. *Wonderful Country* is the title that Tom Lea chose for his novel about Sonora and the cattle-raising people who live in it.

Miguel Méndez, very much a product of the state of Sonora, is a largely self-educated man, and his writing breathes a freshness that derives from the direct experience of living, from a life not unduly filtered through the influence of the schools—although now he teaches at the University of Arizona, where he is a professor of Spanish and of Mexican and Chicano literature. He is also a researcher in the humanities in that university's Mexican American Studies and Research Center. A prolific author of novels, short stories, and poetry, Miguel Méndez writes in Spanish—

although some of his work has recently been translated into English. The border area and the people who live in it form the subject matter for his extensive writing about a widely spread out region where Mexico and the American Southwest merge.

Méndez's publications, with the titles translated into English, include *Pilgrims from Aztlán* (Tucson: Editorial Peregrinos, 1974); *Prolific Humans and Saguaros,* a book of narrative verse (Tucson: Editorial Peregrinos, 1976); *Tata Casehua and Other Stories* (Berkeley: Justa Publications, 1980); *Stories for Mischievous Children* (Berkeley: Justa Publications, 1979); *The Dream of Santa María de las Piedras* (Guadalajara: Editorial de la Universidad de Guadalajara, 1985), translated into English by David William Foster (Tempe, Arizona: Bilingual Press, 1989), *About the Life and Folklore of the Frontier* (Tucson: Mexican American Studies and Research Center, University of Arizona, 1986); *Stories and Essays to Laugh at and Learn From* (Hermosillo, Sonora: M. Méndez, 1988).

It was *Pilgrims from Aztlán* that established Mendez's reputation as a preeminent writer of the border region. Aztlán is the mythical region of the north from which the Aztecs are supposed to have migrated southward to the valley of Mexico and to have established their capital city, Tenochtitlán, now Mexico City. This novel presents the reader with a great sweep of the border country on both sides of the line and introduces him to a wide variety of characters: general Americans, Chicanos, Mexicans, and the Yaqui Indians, representing various levels of society. The Spanish used also varies as we are given different levels of expression. There is the clear, "standard" Spanish of the passages of narration. There is the powerful voice, Méndez's own, which resounds through memorable inscape passages, and there is, finally, the voice of the Chicanos themselves, faithfully recorded, with its sly inventiveness, its wryly humorous turn of phrase, its free-flowing use of obscenities, and its in-group coinage of a special vocabulary.

Although authorial commentary is given throughout the book, there is another center of consciousness used at critical points. This is the mind of the old Yaqui Indian, Loreto Maldonado, once a formidable fighter for his "nation," now reduced to competing with children in a Mexican border town as a car washer, catering to American tourists. Loreto summons up the epical Yaqui past while the reader is being introduced to corrupt, haughty, middle-class Mexicans who indulge themselves in the vices made available by a border town which resembles Tijuana, maintaining at the same time a disdainful aloofness from the masses of the wretchedly poor who surround them. The Mexican middle-class milieu is contrasted not only with Loreto's memories of the heroic Yaqui past but also with the Sonora desert itself, Loreto's former domain, which becomes a personage in its own right. In a memorable passage full of skeletal imagery, the reader is reminded that the desert was once covered by ocean but that the present Sonora desert has "robbed the Sea of its once commanding presence while feigning the very majesty of its motions."

The desert, of course, is no respecter of international boundaries and extends well into the American Southwest. As such it becomes the scene of migration which is central to the themes of the novel. If the image of past heroism is that of the Yaquis, that of present heroism is the ordinary "wetback" headed, through the infernal desert, to the cotton and fruit fields of California and Arizona. Of the wetback and his kind, descended largely from Indian stock, Méndez writes: "From the south they came, reversing the route of their ancestors, in a pilgrimage without priests, without prophets, dragging along a history no longer even worth recounting, its tragedy now reduced to the repetitious, the commonplace."[1] There are passages in which the poor migrants mingle their voices, decrying their lot with rage, despair, or sometimes a humorous stoicism.

As the author takes us across the border into the American Southwest, he sets up another series of contrasts. Wetback and Chicano workers are compared with their American employers and exploiters. The successful Mexican-American entrepreneur who exploits Mexican migrants is personified in La Vieja, the Old One. She runs a chili-dog business, hires a number of wetbacks, pays them miserably, and lectures them sanctimoniously on how fortunate they are that she has rescued them from starvation. The Anglo-American bosses and authorities tend to run to a type: red-faced, asceptic puritans who, on the one hand, are churchgoers and constant Bible readers and, on the other, are ruthless exploiters of their Mexican and Chicano workers.

As the author recounts the hardships of the migrants or takes us to Vietnam, where a disillusioned Chicano, Frankie Pérez, dies a lonely death, he carries on his contrapuntal theme of the Yaqui past. For example, the Vietnam War is compared to the historical struggle of the Yaquis to preserve their independence against the encroachments of the Spanish and Mexican governments, culminating in the great battles against the forces of the Mexican dictator Porfirio Díaz. During the great revolution that began in 1910, the Yaquis are cajoled by the revolutionaries into joining them in the battle for justice and freedom. The Yaquis fought with ferocious effectiveness, only to find that, when the fighting was over, the revolution was betrayed from within.

Aside from Loreto Maldonado, there are other memorable Yaqui figures in the novel. There is Jesús de Belem, the Yaqui *curandero*, who performs miraculous cures without taking payment. His influence among the Yaquis becomes so strong that Mexican officials consider him dangerous and reenact another brutal version of the Christ story. They execute him by lashing him to a very spiny sahuaro cactus. Jesús de Belem forgives his executioners. Memorable, too, is the Yaqui soldier Rosario (Chayo) Cuamea, who, by his ferocity, rose to be a colonel in the revolutionary army. It is his fantasy that death is La Flaca (The Thin One) and that he is the impassioned, pursuing lover. Colonel Cuamea, after the revolution, is spurned by his old comrades in arms, now grown rich, when he tries to reactivate them in the cause of a betrayed revolution. He has the final indignity of growing old and senile in furious frustration and poverty. His death is graphically described in terms of a passionate sexual union with the long-sought "La Flaca." Loreto Maldonado himself finally dies of hunger in the great squalor of a putrifying slum, in his boxlike house made of corrugated metal sheets and old food cans whose labels display pictures of steaks, beans, and other foods.

There is a scene toward the end of the novel in which Frankie Pérez's father, Pánfilo, is shown grief stricken over Frankie's death in the Vietnam War. A friend offers Pánfilo a drink from a bottle of tequila. Pánfilo grabs the bottle and gulps its contents compulsively. The result is that he experiences a sort of "trip" in which he feels himself transformed into a great, black bird, flying over the deserts of the Southwest, peering down at the Chicanos as they experience various forms of injustice. Pánfilo is finally driven mad and is taken away in a straitjacket.

The novel ends in a mixture of voices, those of Mexicans who have immigrated to the United States and now cannot understand their Chicano children. An underlying voice supersedes these, declaring that the Chicanos will become a river of resistance. *Peregrinos de Aztlán* is an unusual mixture of compelling, inward poetic writing and broad satire tending toward caricature. At its best, particularly in those passages of poetic force which deal with the desert and with the Yaquis, passages which seem most congenial to the art of Miguel Méndez, *Peregrinos de Aztlán* is a deeply moving book.

The book of short stories *About the Life and Folklore of the Frontier* marks a continuation of Méndez's fascination with the significance of a border

area which separates two very distinct cultures and with the consequences that occur when these two societies interact or collide with each
other. Some of the stories are humorous, others indignant at instances of
social injustice, but most of them pursue the basic themes that are being
examined.

The opening story, "Mr. Laly," makes its points humorously. Lalo
Martínez has returned from five years' absence in the United States to the
little Sonoran town of Las Coyoteras. He bursts in upon the scene noisily,
full of jokes and displaying his *pocho* Spanish littered with Americanisms.
The young people of the town are amused and call him "Mr. Laly," but
the elders, including his parents, are not amused and think he is making
a fool of himself. In due time Lalo calms down, settles in. He marries his
*novia* Chepina, and they have five children. Now Lalo is respectfully
called Eduardo Martínez. Only Chepina, and in the strictest intimacy, occasionally calls him "Mr. Laly." Though treated lightly, this story touches
upon a social irritant in Mexico, the Mexican American or the Mexican
who has spent considerable time in the United States and who, upon
entering Mexico, flaunts his American ways and speech patterns. The
story also finds a resolution in presenting a reaccommodation to a basic
and original culture.

The story "About When Pedro Maulas Helped God Rejuvenate the Old
Folks" makes liberal use of folkloric fantasy. God orders Pedro:

> "When we arrive at a town, you have to announce me. You will cry through
> the streets with all your heart, telling the old folks to gather together."
>
> "Why the old folks, Lord?"
>
> "Yes, I have come to rejuvenate them. The ancient ones have moved me.
> They are the only ones who pray to me. The rest of them don't even bother
> to remember me. I have come, then, to reward them."[2]

The old ones are then brought back to youth by a special process God
devises, but once they are young again, they discover that they have not
only the advantages of a regained youth but also the added advantage of
the experience of age. Instead of handling these advantages wisely, they
become vicious and destructive, committing all kinds of offenses and
crimes. Finally a general has them all executed even though they seek
mercy on the basis of being grandfathers. God, disillusioned, gladly quits
his experiment. The story is a fable on the themes of ingratitude and
ingrained evil, and the view of humankind is hardly an auspicious one.

"The Old Mexicans in the United States" treats a situation that has
beset many immigrants. The old men long ago left their far-flung towns

and villages in Mexico. Now they gather together on the street corners or in the parks, and they talk. Though they left Mexico because of hunger or because of political persecution, they remain Mexican citizens even though their sons and grandsons urge them to become Americans. They are obstinate. They are now leaving us as they disappear in death, the narrative voice tells us, but they have left behind them their seeds, which will continue to sprout. Implied is the sacrifice that they have made of themselves for future generations. Also made clear is that their love of Mexico has never languished. The story in its clear narration is in no way sentimental, but it is nevertheless affecting.

The story which follows, "El Tío Mariano" (Uncle Mariano), is rich comedy. Cheto López and Lalo Pérez from Nogales, Sonora, have a sow which is something of a runt. They feel that if it had a litter, the piglets would also be undersized. How to have sizable pigs that would yield a good amount of succulent pork? There is an answer. The sow should be mated to one of the large pigs that grow in the United States. The men go to Tucson and find a farmer who has a fine, big boar hog. They know that their sow "would fall in love with it immediately." The two men offer the owner a hundred dollars for the boar. The owner is contemptuous of the offer and insists that the animal is worth five hundred dollars. This sum is way beyond their means, and Cheto and Lalo return home disconsolate. Then they have an idea. They will steal the American pig! They dress in outlandish disguises and go back to Tucson at night and steal the boar, hauling it into their old flivver. It is midnight when they get back to the border. Crossing into Mexico, they are challenged by the inspectors, who ask them what they are bringing into the country. "Nothing at all!" "But what's that noise in the back?" "Oh, that's our Uncle Mariano. He snores terribly when he is drunk." The customs inspectors tell them to wake him up. The two men shout back at "Uncle Mariano," but finally say it's useless. He won't wake up. The customs inspectors finally allow the men to pass in their old car. But when they have gone by, one says to the other: "Not only did that old disgrace seem like a pig, he snored like a pig. You know, even though I was some distance away, he even smelt like a pig. You wouldn't believe it." For all its comedy, the story makes the point of the wide economic distance between the two sides of the border.

Miguel Méndez in "The Death and Birth of Manuel Amarillas" makes an interesting use of time sequences. The story begins with the death of Manuel Amarillas, "stitched, or better, unstitched" with machine gun bullets from head to toe. He has recently come to Nogales, Sonora, with the idea of crossing into the United States. Though miserably poor and ragged, he is approached by well-dressed strangers who ask him if he wants to make some money. He jumps at the chance and becomes a "mule," a person who carries drugs from seller to buyer. Manuel now becomes moderately prosperous. No longer an impoverished errand boy, ordered around by everybody, he now indulges in the luxuries of sumptuous meals washed down with good wines. However, he overreaches himself. He begins to take some of the money which, as a mule, he is supposed to take to the seller. Thus he ends up dead and "stitched" at age seventeen. The story begins with his death, describes his early poverty, moves on to his career as a mule, and ends with the account of his birth under squalid conditions, attended by a midwife in her eighties. His mother, La Remigia, ran a roulette wheel concession. Though the story does not examine the point, it treats one of the prime causes of tension between Mexico and the United States, the drug trade across the border.

"Papparuchas the Blondie" is a paean of praise to Papparuchas and other storytellers who, though uneducated and illiterate, carry on the oral tradition of folktales like that of the cow which seemed able to fly— but in fact it was the vultures inside it which took wing, thus making it appear that the cow was flying. Such tales carry on that lively use of the grotesque which characterizes folk storytelling.

"Ambrosio Ceniza" deals with one of Méndez's primal themes, the exploitation of the Mexican or Chicano worker in the fields of California and the Southwest. Ceniza is a skeletal man and mysteriously silent. He is also an enormous eater. One day he starts pounding his icebox with an axe until he breaks it to pieces. He launches into a tirade about how he is sick of working for gringos like "Mr. Jimmy" for low pay in the furnace-like heat. He declares he is going back to Mexico even if that means hunger and poverty. His fellow workers of the Imperial Valley watch him go with "thoughtfulness and nostalgia." They are men expatriated because of the "desperation of hunger."

In "Huachusey" Méndez sets up a theme which he later develops in his novel *The Dream of Santa María de las Piedras*. The story is a play on the question "What you say?" This question is constantly directed at the Mexican Timoteo as he talks, either in Spanish or in English with a strong Mexican accent, to people in the United States as he goes on his burro through such places as Chicago, New York, and Boston. As he continually hears this question, he decides that "Huachusey" must be a very powerful person throughout the United States.

The story "Río Santacruz" is an example of Méndez's artful prose used in the service of a poetic and humorous treatment of the Santa Cruz

River, which flows from Sonora northward into Arizona. In the story, the river, having come up to Tucson from Sonora, is accused of being a wetback, an undocumented alien. The river is brought to trial for having overflowed its banks and having caused all kinds of destruction, especially in October 1983, a year in which the summer rainstorms were particularly hard, causing widespread flooding. The river's defense is that it has only taken its natural course, and in doing so it has caused all kinds of things to grow and flourish. The authorities might as well ask for documents from the cacti, the coyotes, the deer, and the snakes. Nevertheless, the Río Santacruz is judged guilty and is put in prison. But the river converts itself into a great humidity, and in this form it escapes. The story is a delightful example of fantasy in the folkloric mode.

"Juanrobado" (John Robbed) is another tale of a Mexican fieldworker. Juanrobado has worked hard in the orange groves in the United States. On his way back to Mexico, he buys a doll for his sick daughter, spending seventy-five dollars of his hard-earned money. At the border the inspector says that Juanrobado cannot take the doll across because it is contraband. Poor Juanrobado goes across alone.

"The Bilingual Shoeshine Boy" touts the advantages of bilingualism. Carlitos is a poor seven-year-old boy who ekes out a living as a shoeshine boy in downtown Tucson. His impoverished family lives in the Mexican state of Sonora. Carlitos always hopes he can make some extra money to send to his sister Mary Helen, who is sick and needs treatment. Carlitos is in a jewelry store when a tall Mexican from the north of the country, dressed in boots, a leather jacket, and an expensive hat, obviously a "potentate, a politician, or some great coyote," comes into the store with his girlfriend in tow. He wants the jeweler to show him a selection of diamond rings so his girlfriend may choose one. The trouble is that the jeweler speaks no Spanish and the Mexican no English. The jeweler is at the point of kicking Carlitos out of the store as a nuisance when he remembers that the boy is bilingual. Carlitos is immediately pressed into service as an interpreter, a function which he carries out with considerable skill. As he is leaving the store, Carlitos is approached by the jeweler, who gives him ten dollars for his services. A few minutes later the Mexican catches up with him. He also gives Carlitos ten dollars. Carlitos is ecstatic. Now he can pay for the treatment for Mary Helen and have some money left over to get some nice cloth for his mother.

Miguel Méndez completes this volume of short stories with the odelike finale "May the Dreams Never Die." It is a sketch of Tucson in the early 1940s. In those days the young members of *La Raza*, the Mexican Americans, were poor. Furthermore, they suffered the affront of having their girlfriends taken over by young Anglos from the nearby military base. Yet it was the Chicanos who physically built the city of Tucson, brick by brick, stone by stone. The sketch ends with the narrator giving assurances that for himself and for his friends the dreams that accompanied their hard work will never be allowed to die.

In Miguel Méndez's novel *The Dream of Santa María de las Piedras,* there are elements of expansive exaggeration and of eccentricity which are somewhat reminiscent of the work of the Colombian writer Gabriel García Márquez. For example, one of the principal characters, Timoteo, earlier met in the story "Huachusey," is presumably the idiot son of the Noragua family. But suddenly it is revealed that not only can Timoteo read but he can deliver penetrating comments on the Mexican poet and essayist Octavio Paz.

Early in the novel there is a discovery of gold in the vicinity of Santa María de las Piedras during the early 1930s. The town becomes rich, and the people go mad with avidity and sensuality. Crime flourishes, and the local parish priest, Father Hilario, cannot rejoice because the riches that flow into the church are donated by corrupt parishioners. Father Hilario himself feels temptation and begins to hoard money.

There is a group of old men who hang out on the outskirts of Santa María de las Piedras. They are Teofilo, Nacho Sereno, Lalo, and Abelardo. Their stories compromise most of the narrative body of the novel and are in effect "frame tales," because the old men provide the setting or frame for the stories which they tell. However, Timoteo Noragua and his burro Salomon also meander through the tales. Taking up the thread of an earlier story, Méndez puts Timoteo on the quest for Huachusey, a powerful man or perhaps even a god whose kingdom is on this earth. But eventually Timoteo is disillusioned in his quest when he asks people in the United States about the causes of undeserved pain and death. When the inevitable retort is "What you say?" Timoteo thinks to himself that the so-called great Huachusey is responsible for these things, too. He leaves the United States on the back of Salomon and returns to Santa María de las Piedras.

*Santa María de las Piedras* also refers back to another of the works of Miguel Méndez, *Pilgrims from Aztlán,* when it brings in the figure of the feared Yaqui General Chayo Cuamea. In *Santa María de las Piedras,* Chayo descends upon Santa María demanding recruits. He is met by the Federal forces of General Gallardete. The armies engage in endless indecisive squirmishes. Finally, becoming addle-brained by the ferocious desert sun, the two generals begin to play with each other like children. Ultimately they do not even recognize each other when they meet in town.

*Santa María de las Piedras* is a mixture of realism and fantasy, history and fable. The old men who narrate the tales as they remind each other of the history of the town are delightfully querulous, constantly contradicting each other, thus giving the book its many crosscurrents. In a certain sense, the town's history is the history of Mexico in microcosm.

# 12

## A Creative Burst from New Mexico:
### *The Novels and Stories of Rudolfo Anaya*

It seems fitting that New Mexico, the state which has most preserved its Hispanic and indigenous past, should have produced a novelist who is steeped in the traditions and folklore of that past. This writer, Rudolfo Anaya, is not only heir to these traditions; he also has the personal ingenuity to invent some "traditions" of his own, assuming the license of the writer of fiction. Although Anaya grew up in New Mexico with its large Hispanic population, he has, nevertheless, experienced some prejudice against his race. It was the Chicano movement of the 1960s, which he encountered at just the right time in his development, that gave him an affirmation of his self-worth. He has written exultantly that "a feeling of renewed pride flowed in the people. Everywhere I went, the message was the same: It is good to be a Chicano!"

The novel which first brought Anaya to the attention of a large reading public was *Bless Me, Ultima,* a work of fiction which has both a freshness and an eerie quality that mark it as a singular contribution to Chicano literature. Published in 1972, *Bless Me, Ultima* is on one level an intimate account of life in a Mexican-American family in a small town in New Mexico. But on a deeper level, as in the case of the works of Hawthorne and Faulkner, Anaya's novel makes use of folk culture and folklore to symbolize universal themes, ultimately the clash of good and evil.

An earlier form of this essay appeared in *Puerto del Sol* 19 (Fall 1983): 125–133.

Place is used both realistically and symbolically in this novel, and certain places, with their special connotations, are played off against each other. In the town of Guadalupe there are the school, the church, and Rosie's whorehouse. In the nearby town of El Puerto there is Tenorio's saloon. These places serve as points of reference in the novel as well as contributing strongly to the atmosphere of the book.

The narrator is a young boy, Tony Márez, who is seven years old at the start of the novel and ten at the close. But the point of view is that of an adult mind recollecting the years of boyhood. At the beginning of the novel, Tony's parents bring an elderly woman, a *curandera*, to live with the family. A *curandera* is a traditional healer and dispenser of herbs. Such women were often feared as *brujas* (witches), and many people gave Ultima a wide berth. Tony's family owes Ultima a debt for cures and for midwifery. In fact, she helped bring Tony into the world. Tony and Ultima soon develop a strong affection for each other, and Tony becomes a kind of apprentice to the old woman, learning from her the secrets of nature and also much general wisdom.

The point is made that Ultima's lore and learning come, on the one hand, from the Spanish/Moorish past and, on the other, from the Indian heritage. For example, she apologizes to plants before picking them and teaches Tony to do likewise.

> For Ultima, even the plants had a spirit, and before I dug she made me speak to the plant and tell it why we pulled it from its home in the earth. "You that grow well here in the arroyo by the dampness of the river, we lift you to make good medicine," she intoned softly and I found myself repeating after her. Then I would carefully dig out the plant, taking care not to let the steel of the shovel touch the tender roots.[1]

The novel has its villain in the evil Tenorio Tramentina, who brings upon himself and his three daughters the curse of the *curandera* Ultima. The firm writing and sense of discrimination in this novel preserve it from lapsing into melodrama.

In the collection of short stories *The Silence of the Llano*, Anaya demonstrates, as he had already done in *Bless Me, Ultima*, that he is willing to move away from safe and proven ground. His imagination is endowed with an exploratory energy, and he is willing to take risks. Increasingly in the course of its development, Anaya's writing has represented an important fusion, one which is also to be found in other examples of Chicano writing. Early works by Mexican-American writers seemed to be clearly in the tradition of American literary realism. The influence of such

writers as Steinbeck and Hemingway was apparent. But with the appearance of . . . *and the Earth Did Not Part* by Tomás Rivera and *The Road
To Tamazunchale* by Ron Arias, Chicano literature began to take new
directions. There was a movement inward, displaying the subjective
landscape. In conjunction with this, elements of fantasy came into play.
Anaya has taken Chicano literature further in this direction. What appears to be in process is a vitalizing fusion of American literary realism
with the so-called magical realism to be found in the works of such
current Latin American writers as Juan Rulfo (Mexico), Gabriel García
Márquez (Colombia), Mario Vargas Llosa (Peru), and the Argentine writers Julio Cortázar and Manuel Puig.

This subjectivism and the use of magical elements are both strongly
evident in *Bless Me, Ultima.* That such literary effects are able to blend so
successfully within a generally realistic treatment is due in large measure
to the nature of the subject matter. Regional writing within a rural setting
almost invariably entails the use of folkloric materials. As in the black
magic rituals of Nigger Jim in *Huckleberry Finn,* the lore and practices of
the *curandera* Ultima are inherent in a regional folk tradition. Magical
elements, therefore, are not superimposed but are of a piece with the
regional elements being treated. To be sure, Anaya, having established
his framework within regional expectations, is able to exercise the creative imagination by bringing in elements that apparently are quite of his
own making. Such would seem to be the case with Ultima's owl, containing the essence of her soul, and with the magical golden carp.

The subjective cast of the novel is assured by having a first-person
narrator. That the narrator is a young boy recounting his rites of passage
puts *Ultima* squarely in the tradition of the American initiation novel and
in direct line of descent from Mark Twain's masterpiece. But here again
Rudolfo Anaya is able to work in something very much his own, departing from the straightforward realism of Huck Finn's narration. The dream
sequences in which Antonio's friends who have died appear to him in
nightmares are projections not to be expected in works of literary realism, and indeed they invite speculations quite out of the ordinary. For
example, when these friends are departing from the nightmare, they cry
out to him longingly: "We live when you dream, Tony, we live only in
your dreams." But such apparitional effects are occasional and do not
disturb the balance of the novel.

In Anaya's next novel, *Heart of Aztlán,* realistic and magical elements
are again fused—but this time in a more difficult enterprise. The inev-
itability is no longer there. The realistic elements are familiar ones in

Chicano writing. A rural Hispanic family moves into the city and tries to cope with problems of adjustment. Once settled in Albuquerque, the younger members of the Chávez family become increasingly citified and Americanized, and the father, Clemente, experiences the steady erosion of his traditional patriarchal authority. The men of the family work at a plant where labor troubles develop as a result of exploitation by the bosses and by the tamed leader of the company union. In these manifestations *Heart of Aztlán* is clearly in the tradition of the proletarian novel and of the Chicano novel of social protest. However, Anaya introduces into this body of realistic writing a counterthrust of quite a different sort. There is an effort to fuse magical realism with proletarian realism. These are not ready allies, and the attempt to merge them involves a straining of effort which is sometimes apparent.

The attempt, however, is not lacking in ingenuity. A connecting figure in the novel is Crispín, the blind singer who plays a blue guitar. The name Crispín and the introduction of a blue guitar inevitably lead to associations with the poet Wallace Stevens. One remembers that for Stevens "things as they are / are changed upon the blue guitar." Thus the theme of the transforming power of the imagination is introduced. Crispín is a repository of traditions going back to the ancient Aztlán, but with his wisdom and the power of his songs he is also a transformer in the Wallace Stevens sense.

At one point, Crispín and Clemente Chávez, a somewhat charismatic leader of the strikers, go to an ancient witch woman, a darkened and more sinister image of the rural *curandera*. This woman is the custodian of the magic black rock. Through contact with the electric current of this rock, Clemente gains access to "the heart of Aztlán." Thus illuminated, he leads the people as a counterforce to another leader, Lalo, who preaches standard forceful opposition to the established powers. Clemente's powers are to be those of love and of the heart of Aztlán, the generic elan of *la raza.* The mythmaking here seems somewhat contrived. Although Clemente is pictured as being charged with a powerful current of inspiration, the alternatives he offers are not really made clear. As a matter of fact, in Anaya's next novel, *Tortuga,* which is in a certain sense a sequel to *Heart of Aztlán,* we discover from a letter written by Clemente's wife to their long-hospitalized son that Crispín has died and that the labor situation is largely unsettled. Thus the novel itself remains to a certain extent unresolved.

Anaya's third novel, *Tortuga,* is clearly a more impressive effort. Here elements of myth, legend, and fantasy are blended with the story of a young man's struggle for physical recovery and spiritual redemption. A paralyzed young man is brought to a hospital for the severely crippled which is located in an isolated region of the desert areas of New Mexico. The reader might suspect that this nineteen-year-old is the Benjie of *Heart of Aztlán,* who is paralyzed from a fall from a tower. However, this identity is not established until close to the end of the novel. Thus *Tortuga* stands on its own and is not, in any real sense, a continuation of the earlier novel. As in *Ultima,* the point of view is that of a first-person narrator. The young man's paralysis is so severe that his entire body is in a cast, from which comes his nickname Tortuga (turtle). This binding cast functions both literally and symbolically. When he arrives at the hospital, Tortuga's ailments are not restricted to the physical. He is a thoroughly alienated young man. Thus he faces two powerful challenges. One is to overcome his paralysis through the force of will and painful physical therapy. The other is to achieve a philosophical foothold, a raison d'être. This he must do in the face of the dreadful spectacle of rows of "vegetable" cases in iron lungs and even a children's ward of infants in a state of living death. These specimens are at least spiritually presided over by the mortally ill boy-prophet-savant Solomón, who challenges Tortuga to visit these wards—something the other patients dare not do—and face up to the philosophical implications of what he witnesses.

Tortuga is almost destroyed spiritually by this experience, and his physical progress is arrested. He reaches inward for philosophical support. Existentialism of the European model will not suffice. Neither Prometheus nor Sisyphus—seeming to Tortuga to be essentially subservient—will do as a model of stoicism.

Tortuga's redemption comes from several sources. The deep friendships he forms with other young patients in the hospital reveal to him the possibilities of human companionship. With Solomón he has a special kind of relationship. In actual fact, he sees Solomón infrequently and on those occasions has little to say to him, but in his dreams Tortuga frequently encounters Solomón, who instructs him by story, legend, myth, and symbol. These are often connected with other dream manifestations, such as a recurring First Communion scene. The white-clad girls with clasped hands to their lips in prayer seem the very incarnation of purity. However, this aura is later cast into doubt by scenes of the girls disrobing. Frequently among the girls is Cynthia, a young patient at the hospital who is crippled and hunchbacked. Another person who appears to Tortuga in his dreams as both vision and instructor is Ismelda, the beautiful nurse's aide who loves Tortuga. That Tortuga is able to return this love marks an important step in his recovery.

Another significant element in Tortuga's cure is the mountain that he can see from his hospital window, which is also called Tortuga. When he was being driven across the desert on the way to the hospital, Tortuga was told by the old driver, Filomón, that the mountain had magical properties. The mountain in fact looks like a turtle, and Filomón tells the legend that at one time, when waters covered the desert floor, Tortuga was free and swam through the waters. Furthermore, legend has it that the waters will return, and Tortuga will regain his freedom.

From his window in the hospital, the boy Tortuga watches the mountain in its various moods. Sometimes it shines out incandescently, and Tortuga feels that he is receiving its special powers. The mountain appears frequently in his dreams, and toward the end of the novel, when he himself is ready to have his cast removed, he has a powerful dream in which Tortuga tears himself loose and swims off in the great floodwaters.

The central role that Tortuga mountain plays in the novel points to an underlying theme in the novel, that of the power of place. Just as in the first novel the *curandera* Ultima acted the role of earth goddess in instructing the young Antonio to feel and to respond to the power of the river and of other objects in nature, so do Tortuga's dream instructors bring him into a fraught correspondence with the mountain.

Perhaps here we are getting to the real heart of Aztlán. Has not Anaya drawn upon the Indian side of Chicano culture, that which insists upon the land as sacred and as a counter to the man-made and artificial aspects of the institutional religion stemming from Europe (one remembers the flawed Communion dream) and perhaps of formal philosophies? The effectiveness of dreams as a medium of instruction is also a concept that is central to the thought of various Indian groups. In one of the final scenes in the novel *Tortuga,* the cured narrator is preparing to leave the hospital when he receives a package. It contains Crispín's blue guitar, which has been willed to him. Thus we have the added theme, implicit in the others, of the transforming power of the imagination when exercised in the arts.

In his collection of short stories, *The Silence of the Llano*, Rudolfo Anaya brings into play themes and techniques that he has used in his novels, while at the same time exploring others. The title of the collection itself, which is also applied to the first of the stories, is an indication of Anaya's continuing concern with the power of place. Beginning with *Ultima,* the llano, the plain, has stood for freedom and independence, but it has also, in its silence, represented solitude—as in the case of the lonely, wife-bereft man of the first tale.

As mentioned above, three of the stories in this collection were taken from the novels, but in their new context they supply a different emphasis. "Solomón's Tale," from *Tortuga,* is a narrative told by Solomón about a critical experience in his life. Solomón is seeking membership in a boys' gang. By way of initiation he is told that he must kill a great turtle which the boys discover on the banks of a river. Solomón is horrified, but nevertheless he cuts off the turtle's head with his hunting knife. The turtle is so powerful that it plunges toward the water, even though headless. Solomón cannot hold it back, and as it disappears into the river, it stains the water a deep red. The boys run off in terror, fearing a curse. The next morning Solomón wakes up paralyzed. As part of the novel *Tortuga,* this story obviously ties in to the other uses of turtle imagery. But even removed from this context it can generate an awesome sense of the penalties meted out to those who disturb the order of nature. The animistic gods of the river are not to be violated.

From *Heart of Aztlán* comes the story "El Velorío" (the wake). Rufus defies the mortician, Montoya, and the priest, Fr. Cayo, who cite New Mexico state law in their insistence that the drowned body of Rufus's adult son Henry be sent to the mortuary for proper examination. The crippled Rufus carries the huge body of his son back to the family home, where a traditional wake is celebrated, with old Lázaro singing the traditional *alabados.* There is food and drink, and the neighbors stay up until dawn. In this story the power of tradition is cited against the legalisms of petty bureaucracy.

"The Christmas Play" is from *Bless Me, Ultima.* Because of an unusually heavy snowstorm, only the boys show up for school one morning close to Christmas. The teacher, Miss Violet, is nevertheless determined to put on the Christmas play, even though boys will now have to play the part of the Virgin, angels, etc. The boys are more than recalcitrant, and the whole scene is uproariously funny. One is reminded that Anaya, despite his preoccupation with central and serious human issues, is far from being without a sense of humor, as several of the other stories in *The Silence of the Llano* attest. "The Christmas Story" works very well on its own. However, in *Bless Me, Ultima,* it has an important contextual function. It provides a needed respite as events move toward a sinister and violent climax.

Like the stories in Sherwood Anderson's *Winesburg, Ohio,* Anaya's tales go beyond literal realism but maintain a psychological authenticity.

Some of his characters are indeed "grotesques" in Anderson's sense of the word. One of the best of the stories in *Silence*, though clearly in the Chicano mode, is nevertheless reminiscent of some of the stories in *Winesburg*. The difference in time of publication, however, allows "The Apple Orchard" to be a more "liberated" tale. The narrator, a teenage boy, is challenged by his friends to put part of a mirror on the top of his shoe so that he can look up inside the dresses of the girls. He tries this technique with varying degrees of success. Finally, and very surreptitiously, he tries it on his beautiful teacher, Miss Brighton. But he is caught. Miss Brighton's first reaction is one of shock. But then, since the two of them are alone in the classroom, she undresses completely so as to dispel the mystery. After a thorough look, the boy rushes out of the building and runs in exaltation through an orchard whose burgeoning beauty he associates with the teacher's body. Of course, a Sherwood Anderson teacher—and quite evidently a Rudolfo Anaya teacher—is more likely to act that way than the average female member of the N.E.A. The psychological point, however, is a valid one, and the story—particularly at the end—has a good deal of lyrical strength.

One of the most significant extensions in thematic concern that occur in *The Silence of the Llano* is the treatment of Mexico proper. The Chicano artist of the Southwest has reached out for the mother culture, and in doing so has drawn upon fantasy, legend, and myth. "B. Traven is Alive and Well in Cuernavaca" is a meandering story within a story. The Chicano writer is being entertained by a wealthy Mexican in the town of Cuernavaca. Among the guests are a number of writers and artists. They are all pleasant enough, but the narrator senses a degree of superficiality among them. He becomes restive and wanders out into the night, where he confronts the "Mexico which never sleeps." This is the Mexico of the great revolution, a Mexico which has been betrayed in many ways—particularly by the kind of people now carousing in the house that he has just left. But the narrator feels the real Mexico, out there in the night and stirring.

The next day he again leaves the ongoing party and gets into a conversation with the gardener Justino, very much a man of the land. Justino tells him the story of the "pozo de Mendoza" (Mendoza's well), a tale of buried treasure. The loot was stolen by the hacienda owner, Don Francisco, the *patrón*, who had murdered to get it. It is now hidden in the "pozo de Mendoza," but it is said that Don Francisco can never get hold of it because each time he reaches for it, it disappears. Justino vows that someday he will find it, and when he does, it will yield itself up to him.

The narrator returns to the house but again finds himself wandering away from the guests. He enters an obscure alcove, and there he discovers a dignified old man. By intuition the narrator knows that this is the mysterious and long-dead writer B. Traven, who knew so well the oppressions of Mexico's poor and who was well attuned to the "Mexico which never sleeps." B. Traven warns the narrator against pseudo writers. With this ending, Rudolfo Anaya allows the story to speak for itself.

But even deeper than the revolutionary Mexico which stirs in the night and "never sleeps" is the aboriginal Mexico of pre-Columbian times. This Mexico, too, keeps its vigil and, particularly in the remoter areas of the south, practices its ancient rituals. In "The Village Which the Gods Painted Yellow," Anaya makes an imaginative construct of a secret and surviving Maya community somewhere south of Uxmal. Anaya avails himself of the same type of poetic license which D. H. Lawrence used in *The Plumed Serpent*, and indeed the story has a distinctly Lawrencian aura in its juxtaposition of quotidian life in a Mexican resort town with the ancient, secret, and sinister practices of a hidden Mayan town where the village and all about it are painted yellow. The protagonist Rosario is enjoying himself, lounging around a resort near Uxmal, drinking and "making it" with blond European and American girls. But behind this seeming casualness is the strong urge which brought Rosario to Uxmal in the first place. From far north he had heard rumors of "the village which the gods painted yellow," and he was determined to find it.

This theme in Anaya's writing is one which appears in various forms in Chicano literature. The Chicano writer is often a dissident in terms of middle-class Mexican-American society. This segment, as it enters the American mainstream, tends to emphasize the European or Spanish component of its heritage and to suppress the Indian. In reaction, the Chicano writer, in search of the deepest elements of being, has felt the urge to make an at least imaginative contact with pre-Columbian Mexico. One might take the poetry of Alurista as a case in point. Anaya's story "The Village Which the Gods Painted Yellow" does not attempt to "launder" the Mayan past. In fact, as in Lawrence's novel, the more grimly the Indian past is seen as different from the European, the more compelling its attraction.

In Anaya's story, Rosario is conducted by Gonzalo, one of the few Mayan guides with special knowledge, to the hidden village, where an ancient Mayan ceremony is to be performed. Gonzalo, a dwarf, is expected, in accordance with legend, to raise a pyramid to the gods in one night. When he fails to do so, he is grabbed by the priests and spread over the sacrificial stone. His heart is cut out in the ancient manner. At this point, the priests turn on Rosario and cut his Achilles tendons. Rosario understands that he is now the dwarf and the new magician, and that he must return at the next winter solstice to try to raise a pyramid in one night.

This last tale of Anaya's is certainly his farthest from literary realism. But it is certain that in extending his range, not only in terms of literary technique but also geographically, from the American Southwest into Mexico, he has become an American writer in the hemispheric sense and has provided us with an example of a new and important role which Chicano literature is assuming, that of literary bridge between the two main cultures of the New World.

In his latest works, Anaya has continued in this vein. *The Legend of La Llorona* (1984) deals with the folkloric figure of the crying woman, who is said to haunt river bottoms and other desolate places. This work marks a foray into Mexican folklore that has extended into the American Southwest. In *Lord of the Dawn, the Legend of Quetzalcoatl* (1987), Anaya deals with a figure whose importance in pre-Columbian Mexico and Central America was immense. It has been said that Quetzalcoatl, the famous plumed serpent, was a deity whose influence in pre-Columbian Mexico was comparable with that of Christ in the Mexico of the Christian era. In 1985 Anaya published an epic poem of forty-eight pages, *The Adventures of Juan Chicaspatas.* His versatility in the various literary genres is further exemplified by the publication of a travel journal, *A Chicano in China* (1986), and by a number of literary essays. In 1987 he edited *Voces, an Anthology of Nuevo Mexicano Writers.* In the field of drama, Anaya has produced a number of one-act plays for television and for the stage. Still in full vigor, he can be expected to maintain his creative flow with characteristic verve and inventiveness.

# 13

## The Culture of the Borderlands

No one who has visited the border areas of the southwestern United States and northern Mexico for any length of time can have escaped the feeling of having entered a very special region. As the gifted novelist and poet Miguel Méndez, a native of the borderlands, put it:

> The frontier is a human whirlwind. Historically it is seen as the border that runs from Ciudad Juarez to Nogales to Mexicali, Tijuana and beyond, as well as running alongside of their counterpart cities on the United States side of the line. Humanly, both the settled population and the ephemeral current of people who pass through the region are highly complex and unusual. The concept of border can by no means be confined to the mere fact of an international line. As much on the American as on the Mexican side, common characteristics abound in diverse areas of life throughout those states that form the frontier between the two countries. Because of factors ranging from the geographic to the socio-historic, ethnic, anthropological, and linguistic, the region presents itself to the receptive observer as a frontier culture which is of itself and which operates throughout a vast region.
>
> The fence which divides the countries in no way impedes the spontaneity with which the phenomena native to the area continuously express themselves as a consequence of the special conditions and the historical character of the region.[1]

An earlier form of this essay appeared in *Arizona's Relations with Northern Mexico* (Phoenix, Ariz.: Arizona Academy, 1987), 121–137.

A similar concept of the border region as being a culture unto itself is developed in the highly readable *On the Border,* by Tom Miller (1985).

But despite the remarkable fusion of cultures that has evolved in the frontier areas, the history of the region can hardly be described as having been harmonious. Miguel Méndez has described the frontier as a "human whirlwind." It can also be described, from the historical perspective, as a storm front. And the peals of thunder have not completely died away. This essay will examine the culture of the borderlands from the double viewpoints of opposition and fusion.

From the earliest days of border contacts, stereotypic images began to appear on both sides of the line as two quite different cultures confronted each other. These images were perpetuated in ballads, *corridos,* popular poetry, and literature of various types. They form the basis for attitudes which still reside in the popular consciousness of both North Americans and Mexicans, and they represent that aspect of the culture of the borderlands which remains unreconciled. A brief history of these attitudes may serve to develop a clearer understanding of the blockages that still impede mutual appreciation between the cultures of the borderlands. To the early American writers in the frontier region, the culture of Mexico represented an affront to some of their major convictions. The ethic of thrift and hard work, the faith in progress through science and technology, the "decencies" insisted upon in sexual matters, democracy of the town hall variety—in sum, the Puritan culture as modified by frontier individualism and egalitarianism—seemed to run directly counter to the culture of the Mexico that the pioneers first encountered. To George Wilkins Kendall, an American newspaperman writing of his experiences in Mexico in the mid nineteenth century, the Mexicans' unwillingness to copy the ways of their "Saxon" neighbors seemed utterly deplorable:

> Strange that with a country as fair as any upon the face of the earth, abounding in every species of soil and climate, fruit and mineral, the Mexicans will not profit by the lessons and adopt the systems of their Saxon neighbors. They pertinaciously cling to the customs of their forefathers, and are becoming every year more and more impoverished—in short they are morally, physically, and intellectually distanced in the great race of improvement which is run in almost every other quarter of the earth. Give them but tortillas, frijoles, and chile colorado to supply their animal wants for the day, and seven-tenths of the Mexicans are satisfied; and so they will continue to be until the race becomes extinct or amalgamated with Anglo-Saxon stock; for no political change, no revolution, can uproot that inherent indolence

and antipathy to change, which in this age of improvement and advancement must sooner or later work their ruin and downfall.[2]

This complacency about the physical and material aspects of American
culture was typical of the period in which Kendall wrote and has far from
disappeared. Along with this sense of complacency came an unabashed
feeling of racial superiority accompanied by a corresponding disparage-
ment of Mexicans along racial lines. A prominent American magazine
felt no compunction about printing a story in which one of the characters
was described as being "a ragged, dirty Mexican, whose matted hair was
the model of a cactus fence, whose tattered blanket served to make more
evident his nakedness, an unmistakable, unredeemed 'greaser.' "[3] The
overt racism of the period was sometimes complicated by a split vision
through which certain Mexican families, "the old Spanish families,"
were socially accepted while the general run of Mexican Americans were
subjected to discriminatory and segregationist practices.

An early example of this double view can be found in the writings of
James Russell Bartlett, a nineteenth-century boundary commissioner in
the Southwest. Referring to some of the established families who had
entertained him elegantly, he wrote:

> There are a few respectable old Spanish families at El Paso, who possess
> much intelligence, as well as that elegance and dignity of manner which
> characterized their ancestors. . . . A vast gulf intervenes between these Cas-
> tilians and the masses, who are a mixed breed, possessing none of the vir-
> tues of their European ancestors, but all their vices, with those of the
> aborigines superadded.[4]

The New Mexican historian Joseph P. Sanchez has noticed the curious
contradictions that existed in the various conceptions of the Mexican
held by North Americans. Thus Mexicans were both violent and murderous and at the same time passive and docile; treacherous and de-
ceiving yet simpleminded and easily duped; animalistic and sensuous
while being otherworldly because of their mystical devotion to Roman
Catholicism.

The profound and unsettling changes through which the United States
passed in the second half of the nineteenth century—civil war and rapid
industrialization and urbanization, accompanied by mass immigration—
and the terrible events of the first half of the twentieth century—two
world wars and a devastating depression—have had a chastening effect
upon North Americans in general and the literary community specifically. The result has been a changed view of the neighboring country to

the south, at least as such views have been expressed in American literature. It is, in fact, curious and significant that the very aspects of Mexican life which the early border chroniclers found appalling are those which modern American writers have tended to look upon as salutary and bracing.

As a counter to North American sexual repression, these later writers prescribe the natural acceptance of sexuality inherent in Mexican culture. Against the compulsive work ethic of the Anglo-Americans, these writers cite the Mexican capacity to seize the moment's pleasure. They also demonstrate the evident failure of salvation through "progress" and scientific technology, and point out another way of living in the more earth-drawn life of Mexicans and Chicanos. They see profit-hungry American farmers devastating the land with quick-money crops and contrast them with the *paisanos* of New Mexico who have lived and died for generations nurturing a small piece of beloved earth. To the Americans' commercialized optimism and hurried avoidance or euphemizing of the subject of death they contrast the Mexicans' almost passionate embracing of death as the necessary and functional counterpart of life. The early border writers were horrified at the "frivolous" festivities of the Mexicans during their feast of the Day of the Dead. But to a number of the modern American writers, the Mexican celebrations surrounding *el día de los muertos* demonstrated a fearless, if fatalistic, sense of reality tinged with a profound mystical perception.

Among the modern American writers, one would expect that the Southwestern regionalists would treat Mexico and her culture, but what is somewhat surprising and certainly significant is the number of North American writers with national and international reputations who have written seriously about Mexico. A partial list would include Willa Cather, Ernest Hemingway, John Steinbeck, Katherine Anne Porter, Henry Miller, Joseph Wood Krutch, and Saul Bellow.

On the other side of the border, Mexican writers have been registering their impressions of North Americans. Luis Leal has noted the interesting phenomenon that Americans depicting Mexicans and Mexicans depicting Americans in literature "start at opposite extremes, cross, and end up in each other's camp."[5] When Mexico first gained its independence from Spain after a protracted armed struggle, it had great admiration for the United States, which had set the example of a successful revolution against the mother country and had set up what seemed to be an admirable democratic system. Early Mexican fiction portrays North Americans in a sympathetic light. However, beginning in the 1840s, Mexico experienced aggression at the hands of the United States. There was the annexation of Texas in 1845, the Mexican-American War in 1846–1847 (in which Mexico lost half of its territory to the United States), the Spanish-American War in 1898 (not directed against Mexico, but which Mexico condemned as American aggression in the Western Hemisphere), the landing of the marines at Vera Cruz in 1914, and Pershing's expedition into Mexico in 1916.

One of the results of these experiences was that the North American was portrayed in Mexican literature in a progressively less favorable light. "Thus," according to Leal, "we go from the sympathetic, friendly, likeable portrait of the American to that of a person who is almost always unattractive, ugly, often repulsive, and frequently morally decadent."[6] On the subject of physical appearances, Leal makes the rather amusing point that Americans struck Mexicans as having oversized feet. They were *patones,* and as such were celebrated in a number of doggerel poems and *corridos.*

John S. Brushwood has studied the figure of the North American in Mexican literature. He, too, notes an emphasis upon an unprepossessing physical appearance as well as upon the traits of being overbearing and exploitative. After analyzing a number of works, he sums up by saying that "norteamericanos are depicted as large, blond, red faced, racistic, wealthy, exploitative, overly organized, and lacking in artistic sensibility."[7]

But these images and counterimages, unflattering to both peoples and still—to a considerable extent—current, should not obscure the fact that the two cultures complemented each other and worked together in important ways—particularly in the border region. In a significant sense the United States, the newcomer to the West, was an apprentice to Mexico. This was certainly true in the great enterprise of raising cattle. By the time the North Americans ventured into the border regions, the Mexican vaquero or cowboy had gone through over three hundred years of conditioning in a very special environment. He passed on his techniques, vocabulary, and lore to the Anglo-American cattleman of the Southwest. In *The King Ranch* Tom Lea writes:

> The hacienda's work developed a picturesque and unprecedented type of New World herdsman: the vaquero. It was the vaquero of Mexico who invented a technique for the horseback handling of half-wild cattle on an open range. He became adept at tossing a coiled raw-hide rope he made with a sliding noose. He sat a saddle with a pommel he designed and built as a sturdy snubbing post for his rope, to hold what he caught. He rode a

strong-legged and tender-mouthed pony he trained for the work of herding and roping. He used the branding iron derived from Spain to burn the mark of ownership into an animal's living hide. . . . The Mexican vaqueros became the prototypes who furnished the ready-made tools, the range techniques, even the lingo, from which sprang the cowboy of song and story. The Mexican haciendas provided the primal outlines for the pattern which produced the later Cattle Kingdom of the American West.[8]

A similar adaptation occurred in the mining industry, where from Spanish colonial times mining of gold, silver, and copper flourished in northern Mexico. Again, the incoming North Americans not only borrowed techniques but also took over Spanish terminology and assimilated the lore of the industry.

However, there was one important industry in the nineteenth century in which the influence went the other way. In 1880, the railroad reached Tucson, Arizona, and radically effected the character of life in the entire region. Until that time, although Tucson had become nominally American as a result of the Gadsden Purchase of 1853, it had in fact remained a Sonoran community. All basic supplies, as well as luxuries and entertainment, came up from Sonora by wagon train. An American in Tucson, in those days, would feel totally isolated socially if he did not acquire at least a rudimentary ability to communicate in the Spanish language. This situation is graphically illustrated in an account of the life of the American military under General Crook in Tucson during this period.[9] All dances and other forms of public entertainment were arranged and conducted by Spanish-speaking people, and the medium of communication was definitely Spanish. It was the railroad that converted Tucson into an American city by tying it into the rest of the American economy. But the railroad, though an agent of Americanization, occupied an extremely important place in the lives of Mexican-Americans in the Southwest. It became a prime means of livelihood among them, as Mexicans took over most of the basic manual labor positions in railroad operations. This being the case, the railroads entered into the Mexican lore of the Southwest, much celebrated in song and story.

Though the railroads were an American import into Mexican areas, there was one famous Mexican who used them very creatively and to his own purpose. It was part of the genius of Pancho Villa as a practitioner of the art of guerrilla warfare that he recognized, more than did any of his opponents among the Mexican revolutionary factions, the uses to which the railroad could be put in warfare, especially warfare of the type being waged in northern Mexico. Villa would seize trains and suddenly appear in unexpected locations, much to the consternation of his enemies. And when he and his armies chose to disappear, they would pull up the tracks behind them, making pursuit impossible. Many of the songs about the exploits of Pancho Villa are set to the rhythms of the trains.

Though the towns absorbed by the United States through the Mexican-American War (1846–1847) and the Gadsden Purchase became increasingly Americanized, the influence of Mexico remained strong for many years. Mexican entrepreneurs came into such cities as Tucson and either competed with or formed partnerships with their Anglo counterparts. But, though close personal relationships across cultures were often formed, such early Mexican entrepreneurs as Estevan Ochoa, Mariano Samaniego, and Leopoldo Carrillo, as Thomas E. Sheridan has told us, adhered strongly, in their private lives, to their Mexican culture.[10]

In recent years there have been interesting industrial developments in the border region which appear to be bringing about changes in Mexican cultural patterns. The *maquiladoras,* twin industrial plants in which part or all of the manufacturing processes of American companies are done in plants set up on the Mexican side of the border, employ a great number of Mexican women. These women, sometimes living alone and away from home or perhaps being the major breadwinners of their families, seem to be attaining a greater independence and assertiveness than has been traditional among Mexican women.

Recently a group of Americans toured the new Ford manufacturing plant in Hermosillo. Their guide during the tour was a young Mexican woman. She strode along the assembly lines in work boots with work pants tucked into them. She spoke English well and seemed to have a mastery of the complicated technologies that went into modern automobile manufacturing. She had no difficulty answering questions asked by technically trained people in the tour group. After the tour, several members of the group expressed admiration for their guide and ventured the opinion that here was the representative of a new type of Mexican woman.

One of the important cultural results of the interplay of industries and other economic activities across the border has been the effect of these activities upon language. The cattle industry in the American Southwest borrowed a great deal of its working vocabulary from Mexico. As Edward Larocque Tinker tells us about the American cowboy:

> He wears a *sombrero* and *chaps* (chaparreros), his stirrups are protected by *tapacieros,* and his lariat (from La Riata) has a *hondo* on the end, he rides a

bronco when he works a rodeo, and disciplines it with a quirt. His saddle has *cinchas, latigos,* and *alforjas;* he calls his string of ponies a *remuda* and the equine stock of a ranch a *caballada,* which he often shortens to cavvy. He has twisted the word *mesteño* into mustang, the generic terms for the descendents of Spanish horses, and savvy, a corruption of *sabe,* is understood by everyone and has received canonization in Webster's dictionary.[11]

A number of Spanish words have also found their way into the mining industry, including such common terms as *placer* and *bonanza.*

The reverse process of linguistic absorption in the borderlands has been the phenomenon of *pochismos,* English words brought into Spanish and Hispanicized. Thus we have *lonchería, carro, parquear, gasolina,* and many more. The late Mexican writer José Vasconcelos expressed his horror at this corruption of the Spanish language. It was bad enough, he wrote, that these *pochismos* were being used in the American Southwest, but it was utterly appalling that they were seeping down into Mexico proper and vulgarizing the language. Not long ago, the Mexican government itself took up the cause of staving off Americanisms and established the Commission for the Defense of the Spanish Language, but the brazen creativity of language is such that no border, academy, nor commission can halt the intrinsic urge of language to amalgamate into itself whatever suits its current purposes.

This form of creativity seems inherent in the process of language itself as it works its way through the collective thought processes and imagination of people. But there has also been, in the border region, a deliberate creativity applied to the interplay of English and Spanish in the area. The Mexican-American writers who have created the ever growing body of Chicano literature have made deft use of their facility in both languages. In a number of their works, the languages coalesce, giving a vivid sense of the borderlands as a region where two cultures have come together to make yet a third. For example, the poet Alurista complains about officialdom in the following lines of verse:

> dust gathers on the shoulders
>     of dignitaries
> y de dignidad
>     no saben nada
> muertos en el polvo
>     they bite the earth
> and return
>     to dust[12]

A different effect was the aim of the late writer Tomás Rivera, who presented a group of loosely connected episodes tied together by the consciousness of a single narrator. In addition, the work appears in two languages with two titles: . . . *and the earth did not part* and . . . *y no se lo tragó la tierra*. The two versions appear side by side, and the bilingual reader can appreciate the varying nuances of the two languages.

On the popular level, bilingualism flourishes in the form of the bilingual joke. James S. Griffith, director of the Southwest Folklore Center at the University of Arizona, maintains that the bilingual border joke plays a significant social role in the border area. In fact, it serves as a definer of the area. It also works as a lubricant against the abrasions of life in a bilingual, bicultural society. Those who deal in this humor know that they live among a special group, and the exchange of these jokes makes people feel good about each other.

A typical bilingual joke, among Jim Griffith's endless store of them, is the following: A sheriff on the Arizona side of Ambos Nogales has grabbed a Mexican from the other side of the line whom he is convinced is guilty of robbing a bank. The sheriff, knowing no Spanish, has to make use of an interpreter. "Ask him," says the sheriff to the interpreter, "where he stashed the money." The Mexican refuses to answer. The sheriff then draws his pistol and says to the interpreter: "Tell him that if he doesn't tell me, I'll shoot him on the spot." Finally the Mexican says to the interpreter in Spanish (and in the classic bilingual joke this part would be in Spanish) "Well, I hid the money in my brother-in-law's house. It's under a brick on the right side of the stove." "What is he saying; what is he saying?" demands the sheriff. "Well," answers the interpreter, "he says that he's ready to stand up and die like a man." In this joke, the sheriff, as non-Spanish speaker, is the outsider and "fall guy."

A constant reminder of the pervasive presence of Mexican culture in the American Southwest appears in the architecture of the region. Builders and developers are, of course, constantly presenting us with types of architectural pastiche which are passed off as being "Spanish" design. These houses, as often as not, appear in developments whose street names are in Spanish or what purports to be Spanish. The best that can be said for these efforts is that they represent the sincerest form of flattery. But the real thing also exists. There are, of course, the famous churches, some dating back to Spanish colonial times, as in the remarkably preserved example of Spanish churrigueresque architecture, San Xavier del Bac. The Mexican adobe style of house was almost universal at the time when the United States took over what is now the American Southwest, and the style has proved its durability. As architecture historian Robert C. Giebner has pointed out, adobe-style houses now exist side by side with the later American territorial style, and the two have often been ingeniously blended. But apart from the styling of individual buildings, the entire layout of communities in the Southwest bears the imprint of Spanish/Mexican conceptualizing. This is especially true of the smaller, older communities. A number of these, for example, are developed around a central plaza, Mexican style. The felicity of such an arrangement was eloquently stated by Charles M. Flandrau in *Viva Mexico!* His paean to the Mexican plaza might apply as well to many a Southwestern community:

> The plaza is in constant use from morning until late at night. . . . By eleven o'clock at night the whole town will, at various hours, have passed through it, strolled in it, played, sat, rested, talked, or thought in it. . . . The plaza is a kind of social clearinghouse—a resource—a solution. I know of nothing quite like it, and nothing as fertile in the possibilities of innocent diversion.[13]

The sight of impressive and historic church buildings situated throughout the landscape of the Southwest is a continual reminder that the Spanish conquest of Mexico was, among other things, a missionary enterprise. The Roman Catholic Church, in the early days of the American Southwest, was almost completely a Mexican organization. As it had in the days of the Spanish and Mexican regimes, the church in the early Southwest continued to be a focus for social as well as religious activities. Saints' days were not only days of worship, they were also days of fiesta. In southern Arizona, as Thomas Sheridan tells us, the feasts of San Isidro, San Juan, and particularly San Augustín, patron saint of Tucson, were occasions not only of masses and great religious processions but also of high-spirited festivities which included music, dancing, and cockfighting. But the greatest enthusiasm was directed toward the events on horseback, the races, with passionate backers and bettors, and the various games that were played on horseback.[14]

As non-Mexican Catholics began to arrive in Arizona in growing numbers, churches were built to accommodate them, and the churches which remained as Mexican churches became increasingly segregated. These churches continued the life of ritual and festivity which had always surrounded them, but with the emergence of an increasingly influential Mexican-American middle class and the consequent decline of segregated life patterns, many Mexican-Americans affiliated themselves with Catholic churches in their new residential areas, churches which were not oriented toward Mexican custom. Thus the decline of the segregated church in the Southwest has made the Catholic Church in that area less Mexican. For example, there has been a decline in the custom of the *quinceanera,* the Mexican version of the coming-out party. Girls of Mexican descent would, in their fifteenth year, be presented to society as a group by their parents. The young women would be dressed in immaculate white dresses for the occasion and would attend a mass, which was a central event of the function. Then would follow a series of dances and other social events. In recent years, some priests have been discouraging the *quinceaneras* on the grounds that they entail expenses for the families involved which are more than they can rightly bear.

While it is true that the Catholic Church in the Southwest is less natively Mexican than it has been in the past, it is also true, by another turn of attitudes, that priests in the area who are not of Mexican descent have become increasingly concerned about preserving aspects of the historical heritage of the region. Thus in the 1970s, Father Charles Rourke of the Newman Center in Tucson established a mariachi group composed of Mexican-American teenagers. They called themselves Los Changitos Feos, the Ugly Little Monkeys, and Father Rourke himself, a large man, handled with aplomb and skill the *guitarón,* the big, pot-bellied guitar which provides the deep rhythm for the mariachi band. The group has had many successes in the years that followed.

The old mission church of San Xavier del Bac, established by Father Kino, is under the control of such priests as Father (and Doctor) Kieran McCarty, who is deeply knowledgeable in the history of the region and determined to maintain the historical character of the church. The University of Arizona sponsors tours of the Southwest missions, led by historians and anthropologists, among them Doctor and Father Charles Polzer, S.J. The revival of such customs as Las Posadas, the enactment of the progress from house to house of Mary and Joseph, seeking lodging, is sponsored by a number of churches. Perhaps the elevation of Manuel Moreno to the position of bishop of southern Arizona signals a greater return of Mexican influence to the religious life of the region.

In a certain sense, the sorts of festivities that centered around the saints' days earlier in the life of southern Arizona have continued, but now they are occasioned by Mexican patriotic holidays, which serve as times when Mexican-Americans in Arizona remember their cultural heritage. There is Mexican Independence Day, September 16, and, most festively, the Cinco de Mayo, when Mexican-Americans celebrate May 5, 1862, the day on which an outnumbered Mexican force under General

Ignacio Zaragoza defeated Napoleon III's French invaders in a battle outside of the city of Puebla. It is not surprising, or perhaps particularly important, that some celebrants of Cinco de Mayo cannot say why that date is an occasion of celebration. The important fact is that it is a day on which La Raza in Arizona celebrates itself. In Tucson, for example, there are four days of celebration in Kennedy Park and in Oury Park, sponsored by Mexican-American organizations. Music by various groups, including bands that have come up from Mexico, is almost continuous. Food booths are set up. There are dancing and games. In the public libraries, the occasion is celebrated by readings of bilingual stories for children. There is a much publicized foot race, for which the contestants have done hard training. Cinco de Mayo celebrations are also held in Benson and in Sahuarita; and in Ambos Nogales, the processions and bands snake their ways through both cities.

Prominent through all these celebrations are the ubiquitous mariachi bands. They remain a strong element in the Mexican folk culture of the Southwest. In recent years, this element has been strongly reinforced by the annual Mariachi Conference in Tucson. Well-known mariachi groups from Mexico come to the Tucson Community Center, where they not only give performances but also conduct workshops to which aspiring Arizona mariachi musicians come to improve their techniques. For the past two years, the Mariachi Vargas de Tecalitlán, the most prestigious of all of Mexico's mariachi groups, has come to the conference and given performances and workshops. On each occasion, it has given a special concert in which Tucson's famous popular singer, Linda Ronstadt, has taken part, celebrating her Mexican heritage with strong and authentic renditions of popular mariachi songs. On both occasions, her father Gilbert joined in.

This family performance has served as a reminder to old-time Tucsonans that the Ronstadts represent a strong musical tradition in Tucson. The most popular of the nineteenth-century musical bands was put together by Federico Ronstadt in 1888. It was composed of young men, some of whom were later to become prominent in the Tucson business community, such as Carlos Jacome and Genaro Manzo, to say nothing of the Ronstadts themselves. The Club Filarmónica, as they called themselves, remained popular for many years in Tucson and environs with their renditions of Mexican music. But the group's greatest success was in 1896, when it conducted a triumphant tour of southern California.[15] Federico's daughter, Luisa, who performed under the stage name of Luisa Espinel, became internationally famous as a singer and interpreter of

Hispanic folk music. In the course of her career, she did extensive research, not only in Hispanic America but also in Spain.[16]

Mexico's unique contribution to Hispanic folk music is the *corrido*,
which flourishes in the frontier region on both sides of the border. The
*corrido* is a topical song. If something happens in the border region, before
long there will be a *corrido* about it. There are *corridos* about the Hannigan
brothers in Douglas, about the strike in Morenci, about the refusal of the
University of Arizona to grant tenure to a popular teacher of Chicano
literature. The drug trade has spawned many *corridos*, such as a current
favorite about a drug rip-off, "El Contrabando de Nogales." Another
favorite topic is illegal border crossings and the looming presence of the
Immigration and Naturalization Service, or La Migra, as it is universally
known along the border. The *corrido*, says Jim Griffith, is "the editorial
page of *el pueblo*, and it always has a point of view."

Another musical expression which is heard on both sides of the border
is *la música norteña*. This music from northern Mexico, with its strong
beat and its emphasis upon drums and accordion, is quite different from
the mariachi music, which originated in the state of Jalisco, and the
*jarocho* music from Vera Cruz, featuring the plucked strings of the harp.
*Norteño* is boisterous party and dancing music, expressive of the tough,
straightforward vaquero of northern Mexico when he is in a mood to
romp. In Tucson and in a number of other Arizona towns in the border
region, there are restaurants, cantinas, and dance halls where *norteño* is
featured.

The fine arts, as well as the popular arts, have flourished among the
Mexican-American community. Tucson has a long tradition of Spanish-
language theater. In the early twentieth century the Teatro Carmen was
founded and soon became the center for the expression of Hispanic
culture in Tucson. The best of Spanish and Latin American drama, going
back to Spain's golden age, was performed in that theater. The great years
of the early Teatro Carmen were from 1915 to 1922, and it is no doubt
expressive of a resurgence of Hispanic culture in Arizona that the Teatro
Carmen has been reestablished in Tucson under the leadership of such
talented writers in the Hispanic community as Sylvia Woods. Aside from
the kind of repertoire presented in the earlier theater, the new Teatro
Carmen seeks to encourage local playwrights and local theater arts in
general. Aside from its specific activities, it serves as a consultancy group
for dramatic activity throughout the Hispanic community in Tucson.

Across the border in Nogales, Sonora, another theater has been established under the agency of GAUNAC (Grupo de Artistas Unidas de

Nogales en Asociación Cultural). This theatrical group has set up a two-hundred-seat theater in an upstairs area on Avenida Obregón. Under the leadership of young and enthusiastic people such as Teresa Leal and Rosalba Romero, GAUNAC puts on theatricals and performance art and stands ready to lend its theater for quality theatrical performances.

In terms of the phenomena of the border areas between Mexico and the United States, James S. Griffith has made the point that border cities which face each other across the line, such as Nogales, Arizona, and Nogales, Sonora, are not completely representative of either country. This becomes readily apparent when he says, "Compare Nogales, Arizona, to some town in the American Midwest." "People come to the border," says Jim Griffith, "because it is a border."

# Notes

## 1. The Fall of the "Big House"

1. Frank Tannenbaum, "Toward an Appreciation of Latin America," in *The United States and Latin America* (Harriman, N.Y.: American Assembly, 1959), pp. 29–32.

2. Gilberto Freyre, *The Masters and the Slaves* (New York: Alfred A. Knopf, 1946).

3. William Faulkner, *Absalom, Absalom!* (New York: Random House, 1951), p. 251.

4. Cirilo Villaverde, *Cecilia Valdés,* trans. Sydney G. Gest (New York: Vantage Press, 1962), p. 133.

5. Ibid., p. 212.

6. Henry Nash Smith, *Virgin Land* (Cambridge, Mass.: Harvard University Press, 1971), p. 151.

7. Ibid.

8. José Artur Rios, *Sociologia rural no Brasil.*

9. Smith, *Virgin Land*, pp. 176–177.

10. José Donoso, *The Obscene Bird of Night,* trans. Hardie St. Martin and Leonard Mades (New York: Alfred A. Knopf, 1973), p. 81.

11. Ibid., p. 128.

12. Jorge Amado, *Gabriela, Clove and Cinnamon* (New York: Alfred A. Knopf, 1962), p. 128.

13. Allen Tate, *The Fathers* (Denver: A. Swallow, 1960), p. 59.

14. Alejo Carpentier, *Explosion in a Cathedral,* trans. John Sturrock (Boston: Little, Brown, 1963), p. 240.

15. Freyre, *The Masters and the Slaves,* p. 72.

16. Ibid., p. 73.

17. Tate, *The Fathers.*

18. José Lins do Rego, *Menino do engenho* (Rio de Janeiro: Editora José Olympio, 1960), p. 71.

19. Gilberto Freyre, *New World in the Tropics* (New York: Alfred A. Knopf, 1959), p. 72.

20. Wilbur J. Cash, *The Mind of the South* (New York: Random House, 1941).

21. Ibid., p. 15.

22. Ibid., p. 17.

23. Jorge Amado, *The Violent Land* (New York: Alfred A. Knopf, 1977), p. 217.

24. João Guimarães Rosa, *The Devil to Pay in the Backlands,* trans. James L. Taylor and Harriet de Onis (New York: Alfred A. Knopf, 1963).

25. Freyre, *The Masters and the Slaves,* pp. 181–182.

26. George Washington Cable, *The Grandissimes* (New York: Hill and Wang, 1957), pp. 250–251.

27. Ibid., p. 322.

28. Villaverde, *Cecilia Valdés,* pp. 146–147.

29. Freyre, *The Masters and the Slaves,* p. 193.

30. Tate, *The Fathers,* p. 205.

31. Faulkner, *Absalom, Absalom!,* p. 378.

32. Tannenbaum, "Toward an Appreciation of Latin America," p. 37.

33. Freyre, *The Masters and the Slaves,* p. xxxix.

## 2. Myth Out of Mexico

1. Frances Gillmor, *Flute of the Smoking Mirror* (Tucson: University of Arizona Press, 1949).

2. Frances Gillmor, *The King Danced in the Market Place* (Tucson: University of Arizona Press, 1963).

3. George Valliant, *The Aztecs of Mexico* (Garden City, N.Y.: Doubleday Doran, 1941).

4. The name of the Aztec emperor who met Cortez is spelled in various ways in English. Any variation is at best a rough phonetic transcription of the Nahuatl word.

5. *Calavar* (Philadelphia: Lea and Blanchard, 1847), p. iv.

6. William Carlos Williams, "The Destruction of Tenochtitlán," in his *In the American Grain* (Norfolk, Conn.: New Directions, 1940).

7. Ibid.

8. Archibald MacLeish, *Conquistador* (Boston: Houghton Mifflin, 1932).

9. Williams, "Destruction of Tenochtitlán."

10. James Allen, *Southwest* (New York: Bantam Books, 1953), pp. 97–98.

11. Ibid., p. 99.

12. Robert Montgomery Bird, *The Infidel: or the Fall of Mexico* (Philadelphia: Carey, Lea, and Blanchard, 1835), vol. 2, p. 228.

13. Joseph Holt Ingraham, *Montezuma, the Serf* (Boston: H. L. Williams, 1845), vol. 1, p. 116.

14. Edward Maturin, *Montezuma, the Last of the Aztecs* (New York: Paine and Burgess, 1845), vol. 2, pp. 8–9.

15. MacLeish, *Conquistador.*

16. Williams, "The Destruction of Tenochtitlán."

17. Josephina Niggli, *Step Down Elder Brother* (New York: Rinehart, 1947), p. 238.

18. *The Collected Poems of Hart Crane,* ed. Waldo Frank, (New York: Liveright, 1933), pp. 146–147.

19. *Selected Essays of William Carlos Williams* (New York: Random House, 1954), p. 22.

20. Ibid., p. 143.

## 3. Flag of Illusion

1. Eugene C. Barker, *The Life of Stephen F. Austin* (Nashville: Cokesbury Press, 1925), p. 47.

2. Quoted in Eugene C. Barker, *Mexico and Texas* (Austin: University of Texas Press, 1934), pp. 35–36.

3. José María Sánchez, *Viaje a Tejas—en 1828–1829, diario del teniente D. José María Sánchez, miembro de la comisión de limites* (México, D.F.: Papeles Históricos Mexicanos, 1939), p. 29.

4. Samuel Harmon Lowerie, "Culture Conflict in Texas" (Ph.D. diss., Columbia University, 1932), p. 81.

5. Eugene C. Barker, ed., "The Austin Papers," in *Annual Report for the American Historical Association for the Year 1922,* vol. 2, p. 788.

6. Alleine Howren, "Causes and Origin of the Decree of April 6, 1830," *The Southwestern Historical Quarterly* 16:395.

7. Lucas Alamán, *Historia de Méjico,* vol. 5 (México, D.F.: Editorial Jus, 1851), p. 877.

8. Barker, *Mexico and Texas,* p. 149.

9. Mattie Austin Hatcher, *Letters of an Early American Traveller—Mary Austin Holley, Her Life and Her Works* (Dallas: Southwest Press, 1933), p. 56.

10. Barker, *The Life of Stephen F. Austin,* pp. 127–128.

11. José María Tornel, "Texas and the United States of America in Their Relations with the Mexican Republic," in *The Mexican Side of the Texas Revolution,* comp. and trans. Carlos E. Castañeda (Dallas: P. L. Turner, 1928), p. 288.

## 4. Legend of Destiny

1. Harvey Fergusson, *Followers of the Sun* (New York: Alfred A. Knopf, 1936).
2. Harvey Fergusson, *Grant of Kingdom* (New York: William Morrow, 1950).
3. Ibid.

## 5. The Mexican Presence in the American Southwest

1. *The Complete Poetry and Prose of Walt Whitman as Prepared by Him for the Deathbed Edition,* vol. 2, *November Boughs* (New York: Pellegrini and Cudahy, 1948), pp. 402–403.
2. Mary Austin, *Land of Journey's Ending* (New York: Century, 1924).
3. Ruth Tuck, *Not with the Fist* (New York: Harcourt Brace, 1946), p. 57.
4. Carey McWilliams, *North from Mexico* (Philadelphia: J. B. Lippincott, 1949), p. 123.
5. Harvey Fergusson, *In Those Days* (New York: Alfred A. Knopf, 1929), p. 240.
6. Paul Horgan, *The Return of the Weed* (1964; reprint, Flagstaff, Ariz.: Northland Press, 1980).
7. Harvey Fergusson, *Rio Grande* (New York: Alfred A. Knopf, 1933), p. 143.
8. Frank Waters, *People of the Valley* (New York: Farrar and Rinehart, 1941), p. 254.
9. Austin, *Land of Journey's Ending,* p. 316.
10. F. S. C. Northrop, *The Meeting of East and West* (New York: Macmillan, 1946), p. 219.
11. Bernard DeVoto, *1846: The Year of Decision* (Boston: Little, Brown, 1943), p. 321.
12. Tom Lea, *The King Ranch* (Boston: Little, Brown, 1957), vol. 1, pp. 113–114.
13. Charles M. Flandrau, *Viva Mexico!* (New York and London: D. Appleton, 1926), pp. 279–280.
14. Waters, *People of the Valley,* p. 249.
15. Harvey Fergusson, *The Conquest of Don Pedro* (New York: William Morrow, 1954), pp. 144–145.
16. Fergusson, *Rio Grande,* pp. 125–126.

## 7. American Writers in Mexico

1. Charles M. Flandrau, *Viva Mexico!* (New York and London: D. Appleton, 1910).
2. Ibid.
3. Ibid.
4. Joan Givner, *Katherine Anne Porter: A Life* (New York: Simon and Schuster, 1982).

5. Ibid.

6. Katherine Anne Porter, *Hacienda* (Paris: Harrison, 1934).


## 8. Images of the Mexican in American Literature

1. George Wilkins Kendall, *Narrative of the Texan Santa Fe Expedition* (London: Wiley and Putnam, 1847), p. 326.

2. George F. Emery, "The Water Witch," *The Overland Monthly* (San Francisco) 3 (1869):95–96.

3. John Russell Bartlett, *Personal Narrative of Explorations and Incidents in Texas, . . . Sonora, and Chihuahua* (New York: Appleton, 1854), vol. 1, p. 191.

4. *Selections from Ralph Waldo Emerson,* ed. Stephen E. Whicher (Boston, 1960), pp. 439–440.

5. *Prose Writings of William Cullen Bryant,* ed. Parke Godwin (New York: D. Appleton and Co., 1884), p. 180.

6. *The Complete Poetry and Prose of Walt Whitman as Prepared by Him for the Deathbed Edition,* vol. 2, *November Boughs* (New York: Pellegrini and Cudahy, 1948), pp. 402–403.

7. Ibid.

8. Bret Harte, *Collected Works,* vol. 10, *Under the Redwoods* (New York: P. F. Collier, n.d.), pp. 305–306. (the Argonaut ed.)

9. Charles M. Flandrau, *Viva Mexico!* (New York and London: 1910), p. 26.


## 9. Del Rancho al Campo

1. Tom Lea, *The King Ranch* (Boston: Little, Brown, 1957), pp. 343–344.

2. Edward Larocque Tinker, *The Horsemen of the Americas and the Literature They Inspired* (New York: Hastings House, 1953), p. 344.

3. Tom Lea, *Wonderful Country* (Boston: Little, Brown, 1952), p. 353.


## 10. Through the Southwest

1. Paul Horgan, *Great River* (New York: Rinehart, 1954), vol. 2, p. 886.

2. Edward Abbey, *Desert Solitaire* (New York: Ballantine Books, 1971), p. 267.


## 11. Miguel Méndez

1. Miguel Méndez M., *Peregrinos de Aztlán* (Tucson: Editorial Peregrinos, 1974), p. 64.

2. Miguel Méndez M., *De la vida y del folclore de la frontera* (Tucson: Mexican American Studies and Research Center, University of Arizona, 1986).

## 12. A Creative Burst from New Mexico

1. Rudolfo Anaya, *Bless Me, Ultima* (Berkeley, Calif.: Tonatiuh Publications, 1972), pp. 36–37.

## 13. The Culture of the Borderlands

1. Miguel Méndez M., *De la vida y del folclore de la frontera* (Tucson: Mexican American Studies and Research Center, University of Arizona, 1986), p. 3. Translation by Cecil Robinson.

2. George Wilkins Kendall, *Narratives of the Texan Santa Fe Expedition* (Chicago: Lakeside Press, 1929), p. 326.

3. George F. Emory, "The Water Witch," *The Overland Monthly* (San Francisco) 3 (1869):95–96.

4. James Russell Bartlett, *Personal Narrative of Explorations and Incidents in Texas, New Mexico, California, Sonora, and Chihuahua* (New York: Appleton, 1854), vol. 1, p. 191.

5. Luis Leal, *Melus* 5, no. 3 (1978): 16.

6. Ibid., p. 24.

7. John S. Brushwood, "Mexico and the United States: Relations in the Humanities" (San Diego: San Diego State College, 1984), pp. 3–8.

8. Tom Lea, *The King Ranch* (Boston: Little, Brown, 1957), vol. 1, pp. 113–114.

9. John G. Bourke, *On the Border with Crook* (New York: Time Life Books, 1980).

10. Thomas E. Sheridan, *Los Tucsonenses* (Tucson: University of Arizona Press, 1986).

11. Edward L. Tinker, *The Horsemen of the Americas and the Literature They Inspired* (New York: Hastings House, 1953), p. 96.

12. Alurista, "Mis ojos hinchados," in his *El espejo* (Berkeley, Calif.: Quinto Sol Publications, 1969), p. 172.

13. Charles M. Flandrau, *Viva Mexico!* (New York and London: Appleton, 1926), pp. 279–280.

14. Sheridan, *Los Tucsonenses,* pp, 159–163.

15. Ibid., pp. 195–196.

16. Ibid., pp. 189–191.

# Select Bibliography

Abbey, Edward. *Desert Solitaire*. New York: Ballantine Books, 1971.

———. *The Brave Cowboy*. New York: Ballantine Books, 1972.

———. *The Monkey Wrench Gang*. New York: Avon, 1976.

Alamán, Lucas. *Historia de Méjico*, vol. 5. México, D.F.: Editorial Jus, 1851.

Alegría, Ciro. *El mundo es ancho y ajeno*. México, D.F.: Editorial Diano, 1964.

Allen, John Houghton. *Southwest*. New York: Bantam Books, 1953.

Alurista. "Mis ojos hinchados." In his *El espejo*. Berkeley, Calif.: Quinto Sol Publications, 1969.

Amado, Jorge. *Gabriela, Clove and Cinnamon*. Translated by James L. Taylor and William L. Grossman. New York: Alfred A. Knopf, 1962.

Anaya, Rudolfo. *Bless, Me, Ultima*. Berkeley, Calif.: Tonatiuh International, 1972.

———. *Heart of Aztlán*. Berkeley, Calif.: Editorial Justa, 1976.

———. *Tortuga*. Berkeley, Calif.: Editorial Justa, 1979.

———. *The Silence of the Llano*. Berkeley, Calif.: Tonatiuh Publications, 1982.

———. *The Legend of La Llorona*. Berkeley, Calif.: Quinto Sol Publications, 1984.

———. *Adventures of Juan Chicaspatas*. Houston: Arte Público Press, 1985.

———. *A Chicano in China*. Albuquerque: University of New Mexico Press, 1986.

———. *Lord of the Dawn, the Legend of Quetzalcoatl*. Albuquerque: University of New Mexico Press, 1987.

———, ed. *Voces, an Anthology of Nuevo Mexicano Writers*. Albuquerque: El Norte Publications/Academia, 1987.

Atherton, Gertrude. *The Splendid Idle Forties*. New York: F. A. Stokes, 1902.

Austin, Mary. *The Land of Journey's Ending*. New York: Century, 1924.

———. "The Austin Papers." Edited by Eugene C. Barker. *Annual Report for the American Historical Association for the Year 1922*, vol. 2.

Barker, Eugene C. *The Life of Stephen F. Austin*. Nashville: Cokesbury Press, 1925.

———. *Mexico and Texas*. Austin: University of Texas Press, 1934.

Bartlett, John Russell. *Personal Narrative of Explorations and Incidents in Texas, New Mexico, California, Sonora, and Chihuahua*. 2 vols. New York: Appleton, 1854.

Bird, Robert Montgomery. *The Infidel: or the Fall of Mexico*. Philadelphia: Carey, Lee, and Blanchard, 1835.

———. *Calavar: or a Knight of the Conquest, a Romance of Mexico*. Philadelphia: Lea and Blanchard, 1847.

Bourke, John G. *On the Border with Crook*. New York: Time Life Books, 1980.

Braddy, Haldeen. *Cock of the Walk*. Albuquerque: University of New Mexico Press, 1955.

Brushwood, John S. "Mexico and the United States: Intercultural Relations in the Humanities." San Diego: San Diego State College, 1984.

Cable, George Washington. *The Grandissimes*. New York: Scribner's, 1880.

Carpentier, Alejo. *Explosion in a Cathedral*, trans. John Sturrock. Boston: Little Brown, 1963.

Cash, W. J. *The Mind of the South*. New York: Random House, 1941.

Crane, Hart. *The Collected Poems of Hart Crane*. Edited by Waldo Frank. New York: Liverwright, 1933.

Crane, Stephen. "The Bride Comes to Yellow Sky." In *The Stephen Crane Reader*. Edited by R. W. Stallman. Glenview, Ill.: Scott Foresman, 1972.

da Cunha, Euclides. *Rebellion in the Backlands*. Translated by Samuel Putnam. Chicago: University of Chicago Press, 1944.

DeVoto, Bernard. *1846: The Year of Decision*. Boston: Little, Brown, 1943.

Díaz del Castillo, Bernal. *The Conquest of New Spain*. Translated and with an introduction by J. M. Cohen. London: The Folio Society, 1963.

Donoso, José. *The Obscene Bird of Night*. Translated by Hardie St. Martin and Leonard Mades. New York: Alfred A. Knopf, 1973.

Emory, George F. "The Water Witch." *The Overland Monthly* (San Francisco) 3 (1869).

Faulkner, William. *Absalom, Absalom!* New York: Random House, 1936.

———. *Go Down, Moses*. New York: Random House, 1940.

Fergusson, Harvey. *The Blood of the Conquerors*. New York: Alfred A. Knopf, 1921.

———. *Wolfsong*. New York: Alfred A. Knopf, 1927.

———. *Rio Grande*. New York: Alfred A. Knopf, 1933.

———. *Followers of the Sun, a Trilogy of the Santa Fe Trail*. New York: Alfred A. Knopf, 1936.

———. *Grant of Kingdom*. New York: William Morrow, 1950.

Freyre, Gilberto. *The Masters and the Slaves*. Translated by Samuel Putnam. New York: Alfred A. Knopf, 1946.

———. *New World in the Tropics*. New York: Vintage Books, 1963.

Fuentes, Carlos. *The Death of Artemio Cruz.* Translated by Sam Hileman. New York: Farrar, Straus and Giroux, 1982.

García Márquez, Gabriel. *The Autumn of the Patriarch.* New York: Avon Books, 1977.

Garrard, Lewis H. *Wah-To-Yah and the Taos Trail.* Edited by Ralph P. Bieber. Glendale, Calif.: Arthur H. Clark, 1938.

Gillmor, Frances. *Flute of the Smoking Mirror.* Tucson: University of Arizona Press, 1949.

————. *The King Danced in the Market Place.* Tucson: University of Arizona Press, 1963.

Givner, Joan. *Katherine Anne Porter, a Life.* New York: Simon and Schuster, 1982.

González, César. *Rudolfo A. Anaya, Focus on Criticism.* San Diego: Lalo Press, 1990.

Goodwyn, Frank. *The Black Bull.* Garden City, N.Y.: Doubleday, 1958.

Gregg, Josiah. *Commerce of the Prairies.* Philadelphia: J. W. Moore, 1851.

Guimarães Rosa, João. *The Devil to Pay in the Backlands.* Translated by James L. Taylor and Harriet de Onis. New York: Alfred A. Knopf, 1963.

Güiraldes, Ricardo. *Don Segundo sombra.* Buenos Aires: Editorial Losada, 1952.

Harris, Joel Chandler. *The Adventures of Br'er Rabbit.* Chicago: Rand McNally, 1980.

Harte, Bret. *Works.* New York: P. F. Collier, 1896–1914. Argonaut Edition.

Hatcher, Mattie Austin, ed., *Letters of an Early American Traveller—Mary Austin Holley, Her Life and Her Works.* Dallas: Southwest Press, 1933.

Hellman, Lillian. "The Little Foxes." In *Four Plays by Lillian Hellman.* New York: Random House, 1942.

Hernández, José. *Martín Fierro.* México, D.F.: Editorial Novaro-México, 1958.

Horgan, Paul. *Great River: The Rio Grande in North American History.* 2 vols. New York: Rinehart, 1954.

Howren, Alleine. "Causes and Origin of the Decree of April 6, 1830." *The Southwestern Historical Quarterly,* vol. 16.

Ingraham, Joseph Holt. *Montezuma, the Serf.* 2 vols. Boston: H. L. Williams, 1845.

Jackson, Helen Hunt. *Ramona.* Boston: Roberts Brothers, 1894.

Kendall, George Wilkins. *Narrative of the Texan Santa Fe Expedition.* Chicago: Lakeside Press, 1929.

Lea, Tom. *The King Ranch.* 2 vols. Boston: Little, Brown, 1957.

Lins do Rego, José. *Menino do engenho, Banquê.* Rio de Janeiro: Editora José Olympio, 1960.

Lowerie, Samuel Harmon. "Culture Conflict in Texas." Ph.D. dissertation, Columbia University, 1932.

Lummis, Charles F. *A New Mexico David.* New York: Scribner's, 1902.

MacLeish, Archibald. *Conquistador.* Boston: Houghton Mifflin, 1932.

Magoffin, Susan Shelby. *Down the Santa Fe Trail and into Mexico, the Diary of Susan Shelby Magoffin in 1846–1847.* Edited by Stella M. Drumm. New Haven: Yale University Press, 1926.

Maturin, Edward. *Montezuma, the Last of the Aztecs.* New York: Paine and Burgess, 1845.

McMurtry, Larry. *Horseman Pass By.* New York: Harper's, 1961.

McWilliams, Carey. *North from Mexico.* Philadelphia: J. B. Lippincott, 1949.

*Melus* 5, no. 3 (1978).

Méndez Miguel. *Peregrinos de Aztlán.* Tucson: Editorial Peregrinos, 1974.

————. *El sueño de Santa María de la Piedras.* Guadalajara: EDUG, 1986.

————. *De la vida y del folclore de la frontera.* Tucson: Mexican American Studies and Research Center, University of Arizona, 1986.

————. *The Dream of Santa María de las Piedras.* Translated by David William Foster. Tempe, Ariz.: Bilingual Press/Editorial Bilingue, 1989.

Miller, Tom. *On the Border.* Tucson: University of Arizona Press, 1985.

Nichols, John. *The Milagro Beanfield War.* New York: Holt, Rinehart and Winston, 1974.

Niggli, Josephina. *Step Down Elder Brother.* New York: Rinehart, 1947.

Norris, Frank. *The Octopus.* New York: New American Library, 1964.

Northrop, F. S. C. *The Meeting of East and West.* New York: Macmillan, 1946.

Paulding, James K. *Westward Ho!* New York: Harper, 1832.

Pike, Albert. *Prose Poems and Sketches.* Boston: Light and Horton, 1834.

Prescott, William H. *History of the Conquest of Mexico and History of the Conquest of Peru.* New York: Modern Library.

Remington, Frederic. *Pony Tracks, Sketches of Pioneer Life.* New York: Harper and Brothers, 1895.

Rennie, Ysabel. *The Blue Chip.* New York: Harper and Brothers, 1954.

Richter, Conrad. *The Sea of Grass.* New York: Alfred A. Knopf, 1937.

Rios, José Artur. *Sociologia rural no Brasil.*

Rivera, Tomás. *. . . and the Earth Did Not Part.* Berkeley, Calif.: Quinto Sol Publications, 1971.

Rulfo, Juan. *Pedro Párramo.* México, D.F.: Fondo de Cultura Económica, 1975.

Sánchez, José María. *Viaje a Tejas—en 1828–1829, diario del teniente D. José María Sanchez, miembro de la comisión de limites.* Mexico, D.F.: Papeles Históricos Mexicanos, 1939.

Sheridan, Thomas E. *Los Tucsonenses.* Tucson: University of Arizona Press, 1986.

Smith, Henry Nash. *Virgin Land.* Cambridge, Mass.: Harvard University Press, 1971.

Steinbeck, John. *The Grapes of Wrath.* New York: Viking Press, 1958.

Tannenbaum, Frank. "Toward an Appreciation of Latin America." In *The United States and Latin America.* Harriman, N.Y.: American Assembly, 1959.

Tate, Allen. *Memories and Essays Old and New.* London: Carcanet Press, 1976.

Tinker, Edward Larocque. *The Horsemen of the Americas and the Literature They Inspired.* New York: Hastings House, 1953.

Tornel, José María. "Texas and the United States in Their Relations with the

Mexican Republic." In *The Mexican Side of the Texas Revolution.* Compiled and translated by Carlos E. Castañeda. Dallas: P. L. Turner, 1928.

Tuck, Ruth. *Not with the Fist.* New York: Harcourt Brace, 1946.

Twain, Mark. *Roughing It.* Hartford, Conn.: American Publishing, 1872.

———. *Adventures of Huckleberry Finn.* New York: W. W. Norton, 1961.

———. *Pudd'nhead Wilson.* New York: Airmont, 1966.

Valliant, George. *The Aztecs of Mexico.* Garden City, N.Y.: Doubleday Doran, 1941.

Villaverde, Cirilo. *Cecilia Valdés.* Translated by Sidney G. Gest. New York: Vantage Press, 1962.

Warren, Robert Penn. *All the King's Men.* New York: Bantam Books, 1959.

Waters, Frank. *People of the Valley.* New York: Farrar and Rinehart, 1941.

Webb, Josiah. *Adventures in the Santa Fe Trade 1844–1847.* Glendale, Calif.: Arthur H. Clark, 1931.

Whitman, Walt. *The Complete Poetry and Prose of Walt Whitman as Prepared by Him for the Deathbed Edition,* vol. 2, *November Boughs.* New York: Pellegrini and Cudahy, 1948.

Williams, Tennessee. *Streetcar Named Desire.* New York: New American Library, 1963.

Williams, William Carlos. *Selected Essays of William Carlos Williams.* New York: Random House.

## ABOUT THE AUTHOR

Cecil Robinson found the borderlands between Mexico and the United States to be a natural habitat. He first became acquainted with the region as a student at Columbia University, where he took a masters degree in American history with a minor in Latin American history and completed a doctoral program with a major in American literature and a minor in Latin American literature. From there he set up his own interdisciplinary and regional studies programs before such things made their formal appearance in university curricula.

During thirty years of teaching at the University of Arizona in Tucson, he explored, both in his teaching and in his writing, the interaction of North American and Latin American cultures. He also spent extensive periods of time living, studying, and teaching in Mexico, Chile, and Brazil.

In *Mexico and the Hispanic Southwest in American Literature,* published by the University of Arizona Press in 1977, he examined the ways in which American writers have reacted to Mexico and its culture. Conversely, in *The View from Chapultepec: Mexican Writers on the Mexican American War,* he presented the Mexican writer, from the mid nineteenth century to our own times, speaking out on that great trauma in the Mexican experience by which Mexico lost more than half of its territory to the United States. Here, in *No Short Journeys: The Interplay of Cultures in the History and Literature of the Borderlands,* Professor Robinson brought together before his death in 1990 a collection of his published and unpublished essays over the past twenty-five years. Together, they present his own distinctive and well-informed interpretation of borderlands culture, a field he did so much to define.

ACK 0295

9/24/92

PS
277
R6
1992